Beautiful Parties

Beautiful Parties was developed jointly by Taylor Publishing Company and Media Projects Incorporated

Published by Taylor Publishing under the direction of:
Randy Marston, President
Arnie Hanson, Publisher
Robert Frese, Senior Editor
Kathy Ferguson, Art Director

Produced by The Cookhouse Press of Media Projects Incorporated under the direction of:
Project Editor: Julia C. Colmore
Contributing Editors: Tara Clark, Frank L. Kurtz,
Linda Reiman, Donna A. Ryan, Betsy Covington Smith
Project Manager: Jeffrey Woldt
Editorial Assistants: Jill Hellman, Miranda Worman
Design Consultant: Joseph B. del Valle
Designer: Bruce Glassman
Principal Photography: Dan Barba
Additional Photography: Peter Sanders, Tony Soluri, and others
Executive Editor: Carter Smith

Library of Congress Cataloging-in-Publication Data

McDermott, Diana.
    Beautiful parties.

    Bibliography: p.
    Includes index.
    1. Entertaining   I. Britton, Sandi.   II. Title.
TX731.M394   1986   642'.4   85-14649
ISBN 0-87833-467-X

Printed in the United States of America

FIRST EDITION   0 9 8 7 6 5 4 3 2 1

YOU'RE
GIVING
A PARTY

P icture this: the dining room at a Fifth Avenue, New York, mansion in the late nineteenth century. Covering the table, the finest white lace over a cloth of white linen. In the center of the table, a dazzling lineup of ornate silver candelabra, their candlelight softly illuminating the cut-velvet-covered walls and paintings of fruit and flowers in heavily gilded frames. Between the candelabra, silver epergnes, their tiers of dishes holding artful arrangements of fruits and flowers—a real-life echo of the paintings. The service plates are vermeil, the napkins huge white damask squares, deeply embossed with initials and deftly folded. At each place setting, a silver menu holder bears a card that tells, in a beautiful flowing script, the names of the dishes to be served at this ten-course feast. Waiters in livery stand poised to attend to every gustatory need of the guests. Soon the room will be filled with ladies in evening gowns, their jewels sparkling in the candlelight, and their gentlemen escorts, no less magnificent in white tie and tails. The stage is set for dinner at eight.

At dinner, the hostess surprises her guests with an expensive "trifle," a small and costly present such as a jeweled hairpin or flower-holder brooch for the ladies, a gold cigar cutter for the men. To keep things really lively during dinner, she has arranged for a flock of white doves to be released during the savory.

After dinner, a *tableau vivant*, a scene from history depicted by costumed ladies and gentlemen—a few chosen guests who have been rehearsing for days—striking still-life poses. Or a musical recital.

Elaborate entertaining at the turn of the century had all the grandeur of a command performance, required the planning skill of a field marshal, and took the imaginative genius of a theatrical set designer. One of the best hostesses in New York then, Alva Vanderbilt, commented, "No profession, art, or trade that women are working at today is as taxing in mental resources as being a social leader." To entertain successfully was a task that struck terror in the hearts of all but the most resolute and resourceful. Entertaining today, during the last decades of the twentieth century, is still a prospect that many of us face without enthusiasm, if not with downright fear. Although a person may feel fairly confident about handling a routine event, such as having a few friends over for dinner or lunch, having to plan anything more ambitious—an anniversary, a wedding, a fund raiser, a celebration of a new business, or entertaining the boss—can be frightening. There seems to be so much to do that it's hard to know where to begin. There also seems to be so much that could go wrong. You wish you had a good friend—an experienced party giver with good taste and creativity—who could help you from the moment you begin planning all the way through to saying good night to your guests.

And that's where this book comes in. It will be your good friend, an experienced, tasteful, and creative party giver that will help you plan your party down to the smallest detail, giving you new and fresh ideas—and best of all sparking your own imagination and creativity for ideas—for food, flowers, and settings, so that entertaining becomes a pleasure, not a chore or a worry.

Eva Stotesbury, one of Philadelphia's most renowned hostesses at the turn of the century, said, "A nervous hostess makes an unhappy guest." So building up your confidence is a major aim of this book. Mrs. Stotesbury had an advantage: the help of Mrs. Edward J. MacMullan, who did for her what professional party planners do for hosts and hostesses today. (MacMullan is credited with creating the first rearrangeable dinner-seating chart: a board with slits representing chairs around the dining table, so guests' name cards could be shifted around until the best possible seating plan was devised.)

Another great early-twentieth-century party planner was the amazing Elsa Maxwell, who advised hostesses, "The best you can offer your guests is the unexpected." And she really meant it. Her parties were fabulous: from elaborate costume balls to very funny come-as-you-are parties and treasure hunts for the rich and famous on both sides of the Atlantic. But she always kept in mind her own maxim that a good hostess takes excellent care of her guests. According to Elsa, as she was known to the world, the duty of a hostess to her guests begins and ends at the front door, where she should station herself at the beginning of the evening, to welcome them, and at the end of the evening, to speed them on their way home. Elsa also said that the good hostess

Elsa Maxwell's four cardinal rules for dinner are as valid now as they were in her day:

- *Perfect food.* By this she meant the best of its kind. Whether it's hamburger or steak, make sure it's the finest cut.
- *A cold room.* Nothing dampens conversation and kills appetites more quickly than an overheated dining room.
- *Hot plates.* Gravy congealing on a cold plate is most unappealing.
- *Low table decorations.* Your guests should be able to see each other across the table.

To these we add the following: guests carefully selected for their compatibility and their differences (a group all of the same background and profession will make for a very dull party) and thoughtful placement of guests around your table.

Round tables have come into universal favor because they make all guests accessible to each other for conversation and no one is "stuck" with just the person on either side. And don't be afraid to make last-minute changes in the seating arrangement. If, for example, you've noticed that two people whom you've placed together have been talking with each other a great deal during cocktails, feel free to change their dinner places. They would probably welcome different table companions. If they want to seek each other out after dinner, they can do so.

Just as there is a tremendous choice and freedom in dress and life-style today, there is tremendous choice and freedom in presenting parties. A white linen or lace tablecloth was the rule for the proper nineteenth-century hostess, but today easy-care fabrics are the rule. Or place mats—or even bare wood, if it's a simple pine table—are equally appropriate, depending on the mood you want to create. For a children's party, shiny mylar makes a wonderful table covering.

Matching china is elegant and fine, but sometimes the prettiest and most interesting table is one where compatible patterns, rather than matching ones, are teamed up.

You may wish to spend time in the kitchen whipping up delectable dishes, or you may prefer to purchase all or part of your meal from a takeout place or to have a caterer or a free-lance chef take over the whole menu.

There is no *one* way that your home has to look for a party, except its best, of course. A light touch with flowers is useful and appealing, and this book can help you acquire this skill. Flowers tell your guests a lot about you and your party. If you were a painter, what kind of canvas would you paint with your flowers? Would it be formal and composed? witty? exuberant? casual and friendly? sophisticated? devil-may-care? dramatic? feminine?

This book will get your imagination going about arrangements and containers. The crystal vase of your grandmother's day is still an elegant touch, but it's no longer prescribed by party etiquette. Grandmother's copper baking mold is a marvelous holder for a loose arrangement of wild flowers, however (and can be as costly as a crystal vase anyway). Old or new baskets also make excellent flower containers. You'll find some new ideas for putting flowers together—and for using them throughout your house—as well as some very attractive non-floral alternatives.

Parties today are a lot more fun than they were in stuffy Victorian and Edwardian times. This detail from an 1884 painting by A. E. Emslie, "Dinner at Haddo House," evokes with startling immediacy the mental agility protocol required in those days. During the first course, you conducted a conversation with the partner on your right, and as the next course was served, you switched gracefully to other matters with the person on your left, and so on throughout dinner. It is no wonder round tables are popular now, making all guests accessible to one another for good talk.

Black-tie, Seated Dinner

*O*nly a few decades ago, a dinner party, whether for six or for sixty, was always a formal affair. No need for the hostess to specify what her guests were to wear. A dinner invitation meant black tie. Guests carefully chosen, tables shimmering with silver and crystal, inscribed place cards, flowers, fine food, wine, and brandies—such an affair was the ultimate in grace and elegance. Today, with people yearning to recapture the magic of the past, the formal dinner party is once again the stylish way to entertain. A New York hostess whose guest lists include the city's leading literary and political figures gives only two parties a year—both black-tie, seated dinners with exactly fifty-six people. With seven round tables, each seating eight people, she achieves a relaxed, even intimate atmosphere in which conversation flows easily. Whether your creation is a gathering of friends or a reunion of relatives who haven't seen one another in years (as shown here), the aim is to remove your guests from the routine of their everyday lives, pamper them in a beautiful setting, and then sit back and enjoy the glamour and con-viviality along with them.

A Brunch in Highlands, North Carolina

*W*hen the heavy mist rolls over the Smoky Mountains, residents of the little resort town of Highlands, North Carolina, are cut off from the rest of the world. But no one seems to mind, least of all the vacationers here. For what else is a weekend house but an escape, a chance to get away with family and friends and unwind? That's certainly what the Atlanta couple whose Sunday Brunch is featured here had in mind when they built their mountaintop home a few years ago. Although their house is busy with the comings and goings of houseguests nearly every weekend, everyone relaxes and has fun, and there always seems to be enough time for everything. Even work that must be done becomes part of the general conviviality. At this Sunday Brunch, for instance, though the most time-consuming dishes on the menu were prepared ahead by a Highlands caterer, the hostess and several of the guests contributed to other aspects of the meal. One guest brought a casserole from her home in Nashville; another set up the buffet table; a third, on her way into Highlands to browse through the antique shops, answered a last-minute call for some local preserves; a couple picked the wild flowers for the centerpiece; and the hostess created the dessert. The result of this shared approach to entertaining? A relaxing brunch that featured not only a delicious meal but creativity and fun.

The Piedmont Ball

*A*ll cities and communities have charity parties to support their medical and social institutions. And lucky the benefit committee whose fund raiser has become such an established event that nobody needs coaxing to attend. In Atlanta, Georgia, the Piedmont Ball is just such an event. Held the last weekend in January every year to benefit the city's much-loved Piedmont Hospital, it is strictly limited to 400 guests, who pay $500 each for the privilege of attending. And it is indeed a privilege! Invitations to this gala, white-tie dinner dance held at the exclusive Piedmont Driving Club are hard to come by. In existence for nearly thirty years, it still attracts many of the same people from the old Atlanta society families that attended the first ball. These people keep coming back because they know that certain things will never change: They will always get the best music to dance to, the finest food and wine, and the height of elegance—all in a beautiful setting in the company of their best friends. Nor does the hardworking Piedmont Ball Committee rest on its laurels. Every year there's a surprise theme interpreted with elaborate decorations, such as the "Return to Venice" theme shown here. In Atlanta on that weekend, the Piedmont Ball is the only place to be!

A Benefit Luncheon in Central Park's Conservatory Garden

*C*an anything be drearier than another benefit luncheon in a hotel banquet room? These days, it's hardly the way to interest people in your favorite charity. With today's fierce competition for charitable donations, benefit committees are finding that the best way to attract them is to lure potential donors off to some marvelous, surprising place. Some of the best sites for fund-raising events can be the often-overlooked public spaces that are a big part of local interest and pride. In small towns, a section of the village green or a fascinating old house preserved by the local historical society may be just the place. In cities, the choices range from museums to botanical gardens and even to animal houses at the local zoo. This late-spring luncheon was held in the Conservatory Garden, an oasis in New York's Central Park. Although the purpose of the luncheon was to raise money for WNET, the city's public television station, people were drawn to it not only out of their interest in the cause but also out of their desire to see the "secret garden" of Central Park. And once they were there—amid the velvety lawns, flowering crabapple trees, wisteria-covered arbors, and glorious perennial gardens tended by an army of volunteers—they couldn't help but feel like privileged guests at an elegant insider's party. And that's exactly how potential donors are supposed to feel—as if they've become an integral part of a family. This kind of personal involvement inevitably leads to wholehearted financial support.

A Luncheon in the Historic District of Charleston

*I*s anything as breathtaking as an autumn day in New England when the leaves are ablaze with color? Or more raucus good fun than New Orleans at the height of Mardi Gras? Actually, there's not a region in America that doesn't have its own charmed season. As a native, one may grumble at tourist invasions, but who among us can resist the attendant surge of local pride? So, by all means, show off the way you feel! Chances are that among the hordes of tourists, one or two good friends will resurface from your past. And, as everyone knows, traveling is so much nicer when it includes a hospitable friend in the area. At least that's the feeling of guests of this Charleston, South Carolina, couple, whose elegant luncheon for their old friends from New York is pictured here. In Charleston the celebrated season is early spring. With the azaleas, magnolias, and a thousand other flowers in full bloom, tourists flock into the city's famous Historic District, wandering along its intriguing, narrow streets and touring through some of the fascinating old homes open to the public only at this time of the year. The New York couple, however, because of the hospitality of their Charleston friends, became more than mere tourists. With the luncheon including several other Charlestonians and proudly featuring a menu entirely of local recipes, they were treated to a privileged, insider's view of life in this fascinating old Southern city. When their trip was over, they could really appreciate why Charlestonians believe there's no place like home.

A Kentucky Derby Party

*A*fter the long winter, what could be more welcome than the annual Kentucky Derby? More than just a horse race, the Derby is one of spring's most joyous rites, a tradition dating back over one hundred years. As the band at Churchill Downs strikes up "My Old Kentucky Home" and the sleek young thoroughbreds prance toward the starting gate, even non-Kentuckians feel a catch in their throats. In Louisville, Kentucky, Derby time means party time. Weeks before the race, people begin sprucing up their homes, ordering country hams, preparing for the arrival of house-guests, and resting up for the big weekend. But there's no reason that other sections of the country should feel left out. The host whose Derby Day party is pictured here, for instance, celebrates annually at his apartment in New York City. As guests gather round the television, frosty mint juleps in hand, rooting for the horse they've blindly picked out of a hat, there's just as much excitement in that living room as there is at Churchill Downs. Yet the best is still to come. In the dining room later on there's a surprise cen-terpiece, an exquisite bronze statue of Native Dancer, one of the most cele-brated champions in Derby history. Sculpted by artist Lisa Todd, it wears a miniature victory garland of tiny fresh flowers for the occasion. With the host's attentiveness to details like that, it's no wonder that he always suc-ceeds in bringing all the joy of Kentucky at Derby time to New York! And with each year's party offering a delectable array of Southern food, it's no wonder that his guests make no other plans on that first Saturday in May.

An Après-Tennis Party

*N*o *one wants to go straight home at the end of a tennis or golf tournament. The combination of a lot of healthy exercise, the spirit of fun and competition, and the satisfaction of a game well played brings people together. So, take advantage of the camaraderie. Give a party, like the après-tennis party pictured on these pages. It's not only the easiest possible way to entertain but also the kind of party your guests will appreciate most. After all, what exhausted amateur athlete wouldn't welcome the sight of a tree-shaded terrace, a variety of ice-cold drinks, and some good, comfortable chairs in which to rest his or her weary bones? The problem of what to feed people is easily handled. Most tennis players and other athletes are conscious of keeping slim, and they usually aren't that hungry right after exercising, particularly not in the middle of the afternoon, when sporting events are likely to end. So keep things simple. Put out some fresh fruit, tea sandwiches, little cakes—just about any kind of "finger food" that can be prepared well in advance. With the addition of a few flowers and some sparkling linen tablecloths and napkins, that's all there is to it. The flow of conversation and conviviality of the guests are two elements of party-giving that you won't have to worry about. Chances are that both winners and losers will be so caught up in court talk or tee talk that they'll never want to go home. And you won't want to see them leave, either, because at such an effortless party even the host and hostess can feel like guests.*

Texas Barn Party

*E*verybody loves outdoor parties. But whenever you give one, there's always the possibility that a sudden shower will crash the party or that your food and your guests will bake in the noonday sun. If it's a small party with fewer than twenty guests, everyone can move indoors if necessary. If it's a large, formal affair, an outdoor tent is almost a must. But if you've invited all your friends over to play croquet or volleyball or to go for a swim, not making any provisions for the weather can be an invitation to disaster. A good solution is to use one of the outbuildings on your property. This Texas barn party is a perfect example. On that day the weather cooperated beautifully, except that the food needed protection from the broiling Texas sun. No matter what the weather, use that barn or garage or boathouse or even that old shed that's long been ignored. With a little elbow grease and plenty of fresh flowers or balloons, it can easily be turned into a festive outdoor entertaining pavilion. Even without the steers or the boats, the party will become a spirited event full of fun and adventure.

An Old-Fashioned Tea Dance

"This may be our last hurrah!" joked the Lake Forest, Illinois, couple who gave this magnificent party in honor of their sixtieth anniversary. Nostalgia about their early married life brought to mind the old-fashioned tea dance, that stylish late-afternoon party of the 1920s, before the advent of the cocktail party. And now, in the same Tudor house they had built as a young couple, a place their four children and thirteen grandchildren still called home, a tea dance seemed more suitable than ever, a perfect way to accommodate gracefully more than four hundred guests and the bedtimes of people whose ages ranged from five to ninety-five. And so, adjoining their house, a floral fairyland was created with an 8,000-square-foot heated tent, romantically lit and decorated with yards of lush fabric and masses of fresh flowers, to convey the feeling of an English garden party. Indeed, for the youngsters who scampered about, for the older guests, who sampled the fare on the sumptuous tea table, and for those in between, who waltzed to the music of an eight-piece ensemble, the event was magical.

St. Nicholas' Day Party

*W*ith *Christmas on its way, it's time to polish the silver, unpack the tree ornaments, deck the halls with boughs of holly, and bake wonderful-smelling cookies and breads. For many, this is the most festive time of year and the one that lends itself most easily to entertaining. But in the nonstop round of open houses and cocktail parties, it can become hard to distinguish one event from another. One remedy might be to inaugurate the season by giving that first, very special party of the holidays. A perfect occasion for this is St. Nicholas' Day, celebrated on December 6. Legend has it that centuries ago in Holland St. Nicholas secretly gave dowries to three daughters of an impoverished man, thus saving the girls from shameful lives of spinsterhood. This developed into the Dutch custom of giving gifts in secret on the Eve of St. Nicholas, a practice later transferred to Christmas Day. But every December 6 in Bedford, New York, the original St. Nicholas' Day celebration is repeated, kept alive by the Dutch hostess whose buffet tea table is shown here. At this late-afternoon party, the guests are treated to a house decorated with Dutch Christmas ornaments that have been in the hostess's family for generations. And the hostess serves dishes she's spent weeks making from old family recipes. This annual party has become a tradition in itself, the most eagerly awaited event of the Christmas season. And no wonder. In keeping alive the St. Nicholas tradition of gift giving, the hostess has given of herself. And that's what the spirit of Christmas is all about.*

A New Year's Eve Party

Another year is almost over. It's time to begin again, to say good-bye to the old and ring in the new year with all its gloriously hopeful possibilities. It's time, of course, to celebrate! Or is it? For many of us, New Year's Eve is apt to present a dilemma. Memories of frenzied parties in smoke-filled rooms, forced frivolity, deafening noise makers, too many revelers who've had too much to drink, and our own morning-after blahs are enough to prompt us to stay at home. But that's not an answer either. Who wants to go to bed early on such an occasion? Who wants to watch TV, clutching a solitary glass of champagne at the stroke of midnight, while the rest of the world is out there celebrating? A happy compromise, as more and more people are discovering, is that the nicest, most civilized way to see the New Year in is at a relaxed, stylishly late dinner at home with a few close friends. After all, New Year's Eve is a time both for reminiscing and for looking ahead. So what could be more appropriate than being with those special people in your life who've shared your past and who, undoubtedly, will accompany you into the future? When midnight rolls around while friends chat over dessert, they will raise their glasses of champagne in a heartfelt toast to the New Year. Then, chances are, your friends will be so grateful for having been able to celebrate the evening in such a cozy, civilized manner they will raise their glasses in a rousing toast of appreciation to you.

The Wedding Reception

*E*verybody loves a wedding. And for good reason. Can anything be more joyous than a celebration of romance that blossomed into love and the commitment of two people to spend their lives together? More than anything, perhaps, a wedding is an affirmation of life itself, a symbol of continuity and faith in the future in an often perplexing world. So, celebrate the occasion! Gather old friends and too-distant relatives around, break out the best champagne, and let the confetti fly and the music and dancing begin. But, remember, it's the bride and groom's day. The wedding reception should reflect their personal wishes and tastes, their budget (or their parents'), and the particular traditions of their religious and ethnic backgrounds. Common to all weddings, of course, is the cake. Whether the party that follows the ceremony is primarily a family affair or a gala, a seated luncheon or a dinner for 250 guests, the most dramatic moment of the celebration will come when the bride and groom cut their cake. Also, as in the case of the happy San Francisco couple pictured here, it just happens to be one of the most photographic of moments. So, no matter what kind of wedding it is, lavish or simple, arrange to have the most wonderful cake imaginable. For unlike the flowers, the food, and the music, the photographed wedding cake will be around for a lifetime—an image that, more than any other, will remind the couple of their very special day.

PART TWO

Step-by-Step
Party Planning

How to Begin

*E*ase, effortlessness, and spontaneity—aren't these the qualities that we most admire in a party giver? That's because the parties that are most enjoyable are those given by the hostess or host who is able to make us feel relaxed, comfortable, pampered, and privileged just to be there on that special occasion. We get the impression that the hostess has thought of everything to delight us, her guests, and furthermore that she's brought the whole event off seamlessly and flawlessly.

Every party should be a celebration, a joyous occasion that brings old friends together with new, gives us a chance to share our homes and our lives with them in a very special way. And it offers the opportunity to express our individuality and creativity in hundreds of different ways—and to have a very good time doing it, too.

The truth is, it takes a great deal of planning, effort, and energy to create an "effortless, spontaneous" party. In a way, you could say that that's the good news *and* the bad news. If some wonderful parties just simply happened, then successful party giving would be a matter of luck or of having certain God-given abilities to entertain well. But if you accept the fact that in order to create a wonderful party you're going to have to plan like mad and work like a galley slave ahead of time and that you will certainly see glorious results if you do, the enterprise is no longer a matter of luck or of amazing grace but simply of thoughtful planning and hard work, which anyone is capable of doing.

So let's talk about planning, the how-to that lays the foundation for your party. (And remember that the same elements go into planning a large party as a small one; the only difference is that the scale grows if the party is larger.) To start, here's a checklist of the elements that make up a thorough party plan. We'll be discussing each element in detail. We've organized the various steps into two groups: the *basics*, which must be thought about first, and the subsequent, but equally important, *flourishes*.

The basics
- type of party and budget
- guests and space
- location
- theme
- food
- invitations, place cards, menu card

The flourishes
- flowers and special effects
- lighting
- entertainment
- finishing touches

Type of party and budget
Your choice of party is very personal. Some people enjoy giving only small dinner parties or large buffets or cocktail parties with hors-d'oeuvres. Some people give one kind of party and then want to try something new—perhaps an afternoon tea or a dinner dance. To a large extent, the party budget will determine how elaborate the party will be. It's a good idea to divide your party budget in half and allow fifty percent for food and the other fifty percent for everything else. Within your budget a wide range of choices is available in the kind of food (from roast beef to chili), beverages (from champagne to beer and in between; a less expensive wine can always be poured into a beautiful decanter), centerpieces (from roses to wild

flowers, heaps of shiny vegetables or luscious fruit, or a pretty piece of porcelain), and so forth. Elegant doesn't have to mean expensive; it can simply mean bounty—roses or daisies or ripe tomatoes or some other wonderful thing that you come up with for the center of the table, for example.

Guests and space

Some of the best party givers spend days agonizing over whom to invite and who will get along with whom. Agony is not really in order. This is a party and it's supposed to be fun. But a thoughtful selection of friends who you think will mix well is essential to the success of your party. If you find as you make up your guest list that your party is growing beyond the capacity of your home, you may consider cutting back on your list or having your party outside your home.

The space must fit the number of guests. Guests shouldn't be overwhelmed by finding themselves at a party that is being held in a room that is too large. People like to be close together at a party; it's easier to make conversation that way. Too much space can be deadly. It's easier to open a conversation at a cocktail party, for instance, if you walk into a room where groups of people are only an arm's length away than if they are spread out over a vast area. Nor, of course, should people be crammed into a space that is too small. When figuring out the amount of space that you need for a specific number of guests around a dining table indoors, the rule of thumb is to allow 10 square feet per person. This includes the table, place for a chair, and passage space for the server. In a tent, where you must work around poles, more space is needed—about 15 square feet per person. So for a table of ten indoors, allow about 100 square feet; in a tent, the same table of ten requires about 150 square feet. This is useful for determining what size tent to rent for an outdoor party. Those who rent tents often get one a size larger than needed. Again, too much space or too little space is a mistake whether the party's outdoors or indoors.

It's also important to use the chosen party space effectively. For instance, if you're having a crowd in for cocktails and you want them to use all of the rooms on one floor of your home rather than to congregate in only one or two rooms, you have to lure them into the other rooms by putting another bar or a food table in them so there is a reason for guests to go into them. Once they've gone in, some guests will remain in each.

Location

If, for whatever reason, you decide to take your party out of your home (you may simply want to surprise your guests with a marvelous new location), it's time to go shopping for places. Major cities have a plethora of places available to rent for parties: historical mansions, town houses, lofts, penthouses, as well as private rooms in restaurants and special rooms in hotels. Smaller cities and communities may have some unusual spaces available. Or you may be limited to a local hotel, inn, or restaurant, or even to a VFW hall. No matter—with the right use of materials, any of these can be made to look festive and beautiful.

Theme

There are those who feel that the most memorable parties have a theme, some central point around which to plan. It may be an event involving a guest or yourself—a birthday, a new job, an engagement, an anniversary, moving away, a cruise to Australia, or any other personal event or experience that inspires you to make a celebration. Or the theme may be based on a holiday—Election Day, Christmas, New Year's Eve, the Fourth of July, Easter, Halloween, and so forth. A theme makes party planning easier; it narrows down the other choices—everything from food to decor to color to materials.

Food

The decision of who prepares the food—a caterer or some other food service, or you and your guests—depends on the type of party, the location, the number of guests invited, whether you enjoy cooking, and your budget. Obviously, there are many possibilities. You might want to do a combination of things. For a smaller party, you might want to prepare some dishes yourself and buy some others already prepared from a good takeout place. Or you might want to leave the whole menu in the hands of

If it's an extra special event, surprise your guests with a marvelous new location. For a day, be the proprietor of a stately town house. Or how about a disco, a private railroad car, an historic landmark, a casino, lighthouse, vineyard, botannical garden, a former brothel, Mississippi riverboat—the possibilities are endless.

an inspired caterer. Finding the right caterer may mean doing a bit of research—asking friends whom they've used and liked, or interviewing caterers who advertise in your area. A caterer should be willing to let you sample the food that will be served at your party while the party is still in the planning stages. If not, find another caterer. You don't want any unpleasant surprises on the day of your party when it's too late to make changes. If the caterer is doing another party some time before yours, it may be possible for you to sample some of that party's dishes. Caterers will ask for a certain amount of their fee in advance, usually fifty percent, with the balance to be paid by the end of the party. The caterer will also provide any extra serving help you may need, as well as rental china, tables, and chairs.

Invitations, place cards, menu card
Once you've confirmed the availability of the location for your party (if it's to be held outside your home) and cleared the caterer's dates (if necessary), it's time to send out the invitations. Invitations are not just a detail; they're vital. They herald your party and alert your guests to set aside the day and the time. Invitations should be special, to let your guests know that your party will be special and that it's something they don't want to miss. If you wish, you can begin to build your party theme with invitations. There are wonderful invitations on the market now—everything from shiny mylar to ribbon-laced, with a wide choice of custom printing available as well. Many stationers can recommend calligraphers who can address your envelopes or write out your invitations in a beautiful and distinctive way. That old standby, the formal white engraved invitation, is enjoying a comeback too. It's important to follow up word of mouth invitations—made over the phone or in person—with reminder cards. And do yourself a favor and always request an answer; with its vague implications, "regrets only" is bound to be a directive you'll regret. So often when people see "regrets only" they completely forget to let you know when they can't come, so there you are, assuming that all fifty will show up for your cocktail party and only twenty appear. That means you've had to prepare and pay for ice, hors-d'oeuvres, liquor, and extra help that you don't need.

Menu cards, though not essential, are a nice touch. They provide your guests with an additional conversation gambit and also help them to monitor their appetites for the meal, so that they can save room for that wonderful dessert you've planned. Menu cards also tell guests whether a first course is just that or is actually the main part of the meal. Pretty china stands can be purchased that can be written on over and over again, or you may want to write out (or have a calligrapher write out) a one-use-only menu card.

Place cards help everyone: The hostess doesn't have to remember the details of where everyone is to sit, and the guests know that some thought has been given to where they are to be placed. Some hostesses prefer writing out a seating plan ahead of time and directing guests to their spots from it, but most probably prefer using place cards. Guests probably prefer this method also, because then they can find their spots independently—instead of having to wait on line to ask the hostess where to sit.

Remember that a place card may be just that—a white, folded-over card with a person's name inscribed on the front—or it may be an invention of your fertile imagination. A hostess in a present-giving mood might want to wrap a small trinket in pretty paper, tie on a name tag, and use the party favors to indicate where each guest should sit. Another possibility might be to put small picture frames (to be taken home later), one at each place setting, with the name of the guest written on a piece of paper or a card inserted in the frame.

Planning a fund-raising party brings out the hidden collective talents of a benefit committee. From the outset, the objectives are clear: to meet, if not exceed, a financial goal by attracting the greatest number of donors at the lowest feasible cost. One way to compensate for a minimal budget is to find a location that will attract people for its novelty. Though you can always count on a dependable group of loyal supporters of your cause to show up for a party in a routine gathering spot, the trick is to lure the less committed. A "secret garden," nestled in the heart of Manhattan, is what brought country-starved contributors to New York's public television station to this idyllic setting.

45

A statue inspired by Frances Hodgson Burnett's book The Secret Garden *in the Conservatory Garden of Manhattan's Central Park. It was contributed by neighborhood-proud residents and dedicated to the children of the City of New York. Yearly donations keep the garden open to flower lovers and young people year round. Here, a simple reception of thanks to donors is given by the Garden Committee when both annuals and perennials are at their peak.*

One wife of a Washington diplomat delights her friends at the fabulous "ladies' luncheons" she gives with this unique way of assigning their seats at the table: As each guest arrives, she (the guest) takes a flower out of a basket proffered by her hostess. At the lunch table, each guest matches up her flower with the flower in the little bud vase at a place setting.

For a large party—with more than two tables of six to ten people each—it's necessary to have table cards that indicate the table that each person is assigned to. These can be handed out to guests as they arrive at the party,

or they can be placed in some prominent location, where people can pick them up during the cocktail hour.

With the basic planning under way, it's time to elaborate on the theme, plan the colors and flowers, check the lighting, think about entertainment, and really make your party come to life. Because the theme is the element that unifies the whole party, and because there are so many theme possibilities, we turn now to an in-depth discussion of this topic.

The Plan Unfolds

*B*efore you do another thing, get yourself some kind of notebook and start keeping a party record. It's no coincidence that the best party givers keep careful records of their festivities, including the guests who attended, the menus, drinks, and wines served, the quantities of food, the seating plan, with comments on what worked and what didn't and improvements that could be made the next time. Over the years, this will serve as your record of whom you've entertained, who sat where, and who was fed what (useful when one wants to avoid being thought of as the "hostess who always serves blanquette de veau"). This notebook also will perform an inspirational function: You can repeat a successful menu and decor as long as the cast of characters is different.

DEVELOPING A THEME

We mentioned earlier that party planning falls into place much more easily if it's based on a theme, and that many themes are inspired by personal events or holidays or by changing seasons and colors. When creating a theme for your party, remember the dictum "Form follows function." The purpose of your party and the season will guide you in your choice of colors and materials as well as menu. Just as you wouldn't wear a woolen suit in July, so you wouldn't dress your table in dark colors and fabrics more suitable for cold weather. The purpose of the party will also help you in choosing a casual or more formal look. Casual can still mean elegant, but it also means whimsy and fun. In floral terms, casual means a basket of wild flowers, daisies, or potted geraniums; a crystal bowl filled with full-blown roses or peonies is formal. Both are enchanting to the eye, but what is the party all about and what kind of mood are you trying to achieve?

The most important thing to keep in mind, when planning your theme and carrying it out, is to know when to stop—when less is more. Achieving simplicity is something that takes practice, but the most inspired decor is one that has not been overdone or overworked. Simplicity doesn't necessarily imply sparseness. You can achieve simplicity with bounty. Using a lot of one thing with a lavish hand can look ample and yet simple—and very effective.

Here are some thoughts on creating themes for special occasions. They should help you to come up with your own distinctive ideas.

A birthday party

You're never too old or too young to celebrate a birthday—your own or someone else's. Birthday parties are the ideal occasions to give a really personal party, one that will mean a great deal to the one whose birthday it is. The parents of one teenage boy, too old for the traditional "kiddie" party with cartoons and clowns but too young for an unchaperoned evening on the town with friends, came up with a brilliant idea: a Roaring Twenties party for the birthday boy and one hundred of his friends. Sounds like potential bedlam? It wasn't. Everyone was instructed to come dressed as a character out of that flashy decade. At the party, the guests had their pictures taken (by a hired photographer) in front of a rented vintage-1920s car and later took the photos home as mementos. The kids had a bang-up time, felt glamorous and sophisticated in their "adult" party clothes and guises—much too grown up to be anything but model guests.

One of the most elaborately celebrated birthdays in recent memory relied on a lot of very simple ingredients to make it special and personal. For the seventy-fifth birthday of John H. Heinz, scion of Heinz 57 Varieties (tomato ketchup, canned vegetables), party planner Peggy Mulholland transformed the garden of the Heinzes' New York City town house into a country garden as the setting for a dinner dance for 400. She covered the round dining tables with burlap and created centerpieces of large steel colanders filled with miniature vegetables, with a magnum of Perrier-Jouet champagne at the center of each colander. Giant mushroom caps served as holders for menu cards, and large artichokes, their cores hollowed out, held twinkling votive candles around the centerpiece. She wound long tomato vines, with their tomatoes, around the tent poles (all the tables were sheltered under huge tents) and garlanded the iron railings overlooking the river with vines strung with the same kinds of miniature vegetables. Shows what can be done with humble ingredients if you use your imagination and creativity! The point is, the results were extremely elegant, and elegant doesn't have to mean roses in cut crystal on moire tablecloths.

Holiday celebrations
Holidays call forth memories from your childhood, and of your family's particular way of celebrating them. It's nice to carry on these traditions in your own home, in an updated way. For instance, what does the Fourth of July bring to mind? Is it memories of sparklers and rockets? The red-white-and-blue? Apple pie?

Topiary animals and other fanciful shapes become true centerpieces for theme parties. This two-foot-high Jack Rabbit reigns from a dining-room sideboard on Easter Sunday while family and guests savor the Lemon Bavarian Cream dessert prepared for the occasion. Florists love a special assignment like this one, but if you have an artistic bent, it is easy to assemble yourself: Sphagnum moss covers a chicken-wire frame, and the rabbit sits on a Styrofoam base covered with boxwood and fern; his whiskers are straw, the eyes glass pebbles painted pink.

How about a centerpiece of cornflowers, daisies, and sweetheart roses in a pretty basket, with sparklers and small American flags poking out from the edges? Your tablecloth could be red and white gingham, the napkins alternating red and blue around the table. Or you could have a white cloth with red and blue gingham napkins, or a red and a blue bandanna knotted into a free-form bow, one for each guest at a Glorious Fourth clambake. Untied, one bandanna goes over the knees; the other is tied around the neck.

Keep an eye out for unexpected uses of simple objects. Giant mushroom caps, slitted across the top, were used as menu-card holders at a birthday celebration with an "Old MacDonald's Farm" theme.

Another approach is to omit the floral centerpiece and have a giant apple pie in the center of the table, one that is large enough to feed all the guests. You could twine a circle of daisies, cornflowers, and poppies around it or ring it with small glass canisters filled with flour, two or three hand-carved rolling pins, and cinnamon sticks. Then scatter star anise around the arrangement. At the end of the meal, the pie becomes dessert.

At the same elaborate "barnyard" party, the round tables twinkled with the lights from votive candles nestled inside hollowed-out artichokes.

What kinds of childhood memories does Easter conjure up? Marshmallow ducks and chocolate rabbits? Jelly beans? Easter bonnets and spring gardens? Why not put

Children of all ages love birthday celebrations. Children of all ages also love pretending to be someone else, and, if they are in their early teens, pretending to be grown up. The New Jersey couple whose son was turning fourteen had this in mind when they planned a costume party with a Roaring Twenties theme. They rented a vintage-1920s car and hired a photographer to take pictures of the kids posing as flappers and ingenues, gangsters and robber barons. Their expressions told the story: Those of the "awkward age" are capable of having a grand time, too.

small pots of miniature daffodils and grape hyacinths in the center of your Easter table (with dishes under each pot), or group them together in a basket? Or you could have your florist make a topiary rabbit out of chicken wire filled with boxwood and put the rabbit on a moss-covered "lawn" (Styrofoam underneath) that is plastered with tulips, freesias, and daffodils. Or simply fill a beautiful porcelain bowl with hand-colored Easter eggs and fill the

spaces between the eggs with bunches of baby's breath, and instead of using place cards, spell out guests' names with jelly beans.

Christmas is when your whole house can become the background for a special Christmas party, from the dining table to the tree to the entranceway, fireplace mantel, window frames, and banisters. One particularly imaginative friend of ours does up her front door like a giant

For a Fourth of July party: Add sparklers to a basket arrangement of summer garden flowers.

silky fabric (plaid or plain) to the desired width and then finishing off the edges with a seam. She also uses the ribbon to drape around a hall mirror, the front door, or along the mantel. Topiary trees make ravishing center-of-table decorations. You or your florist can make them from Styrofoam balls, one on top of the other with a space between, stuck onto a rod painted green and held in place in a pot filled with plaster of paris. Tiny pieces

present by wrapping it from top to bottom and side to side with a wide ribbon, then tying a giant bow at the top of the frame. Because really wide ribbon is nearly impossible to find, she makes her own by cutting a pretty,

Festive holiday touch: Decorate your front door to look like a giant Christmas package.

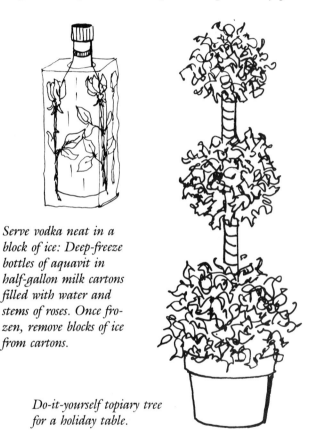

Serve vodka neat in a block of ice: Deep-freeze bottles of aquavit in half-gallon milk cartons filled with water and stems of roses. Once frozen, remove blocks of ice from cartons.

Do-it-yourself topiary tree for a holiday table.

of boxwood are then inserted into the Styrofoam, creating a green background. At intervals, insert tiny white or pink roses, each in its own aqua pick. Then wrap green cloth around the base of the "tree." Evergreen rope looped across mantels can be hung with miniature Christmas lights and small Christmas-tree balls. Secure the same evergreen rope around a banister with lush velvet ribbon.

One of the most attractive examples of how every room in the house comes into play at Christmas is that of the annual Christmas party given for the staff of the Swedish Embassy in Washington, D.C., by the Swedish ambassador and his wife, Countess Ulla Wachmeister. It's a kitchen buffet, where guests help themselves to hearty Swedish dishes from huge pots, all wrapped in gingham and kitchen toweling, right on the stove. Bottles of aquavit are frozen into blocks of ice. Then, dishes in hand, guests fan out to the rest of the house. At the end of the party, everyone is sent home with a gingerbread man or woman, inscribed in icing with each person's name.

Changing seasons
What better excuse for a party—or theme for one—than the coming of fall. The vegetable garden or local market yields a bounty of squashes, pumpkins, and corn (both the edible and decorative kind), and the fall leaves are a party all by themselves. All of these elements can be used in an artful way on a dining table. Grapes are in abundance, too, and look beautiful piled high on a cake stand, then allowed to spill over the edges. The arrangement is even prettier when ivy tendrils fan out from the edges and run onto the table and tiny sickle pears circle the stand. This is another centerpiece that your guests will love to nibble at by the end of dinner, so help them by getting only seedless grapes and precutting them into small bunches.

With a few simple props, you can turn an ordinary get-together into a party with flair. Add your own personal touch to an impromptu Oriental take-out dinner. Have on hand for such occasions lacquer plates and chopsticks, a few imported paper noisemakers and a chinoiserie-patterned tablecloth or napkins. To add whimsy to the theme, turn an everyday glass "rose" bowl into an aquarium with Scotch broom and a few goldfish from a nearby dime store. For a Mexican dinner a supply of candles and napkins in "hot" colors would add authenticity, as would a red checker cloth and a straw-wrapped bottle of Chianti to an after-the-movies Italian-American pizza.

Color me a party
A color scheme can also make a lively theme. Just think of all the things you can do with pink, for instance, a color that instantly signals "party." Along with pink flowers, candles, and table linens you can use "pink things" such as cotton candy, bubble gum, balloons, and pink candy hearts. For another example, see the illustrated centerpiece on page 62 in which large boxes are covered with colorful paper and marked to look like giant building blocks for grown-ups, then stacked at a crazy angle. Their bright fiesta colors might inspire a Tex-Mex dinner served on equally colorful pottery plates.

A simple but effective arrangement to go with a fall menu: purple grapes and tiny sickle pears on a cake stand. Even prettier with tendrils of ivy spilling out onto the table.

Black-and-white has inspired more than one fabulous party. One of the most memorable was Truman Capote's black-and-white masked ball in 1966 at New York's Plaza Hotel. More recently, the exclusive Piedmont Ball at the Driving Club in Atlanta based its design on a black-and-white harlequin theme. The pots of paperwhite narcissus in the center of each table were wrapped in white paper bags tied at the top with black ribbons; the white napkins and white tablecloths held candlesticks in a black-and-white harlequin design that was echoed by the table mats and the chair backs.

At a private party in Westchester, a black-and-white theme carried through to the food. Cocktail hors-d'oeuvres were sushi in an amazing array of black-and-white combinations. Dinner began with pasta topped with a shaving of black truffles and ended with a dark-chocolate cake and white-chocolate mousse.

Sharing some of your favorite things

A theme may also come from something you love: prize roses or sunflowers you grow, a particular kind of porcelain you collect, some game birds you've shot for dinner, or a salmon you've caught on a fishing trip and brought triumphantly home.

One talented New York hostess, Janet Yaseen, has been known to plan her menu and dinner-table decor around a condiment: ginger. Because she has a beautiful collection of Oriental *objets d'art*, she uses a few of them down the center of her long table: porcelain figurines, a delicate bowl filled with pieces of crystallized ginger, with large ginger jars in the background, on the sideboard. At least several of the dishes on her menu contain ginger, such as the delectable lobster in ginger sauce she serves as a first course. After-dinner demitasse cups are set up on a lacquered table holding an exquisite miniature porcelain pagoda. Bending over cups and pagoda is a single branch of quince in a small ginger jar.

Perhaps you've just bought a painting and want to show it off. On page 60 you'll see flower designer Leonard Tharp's arrangement of water lilies in front of a modern painting to highlight the art, one that could be followed up with, say, a red tablecloth and blue and green napkins, all echoing the colors of the painting. Similarly, your own painting will inspire your use of flowers and colors on your table.

Sharing in the go-for-broke Christmas fantasy created for this family living room, a hand-carved swan basks in a profusion of echeveria, African violets, and anemones on an English country table. But upstaging him is the huge evergreen in a blaze of scarlet and glitter. The owner wanted the Christmas tree to be "classic and unusual at the same time." So, Houston-based floral designer Leonard Tharp made use of the family's cherished antique tin ornaments, mixing them unconventionally with masses of poinsettias, to create a truly sumptuous look. Tharp, who is known for bold design, feels holiday decor needn't be confined to traditional arrangements. "Make use of expected materials in dramatically new ways, to establish impact and punch," he says. The result: a country-style room transformed into an exotic fairyland right out of The Nutcracker.

Winter
Take the chill out of winter with the warmth of primary colors. Gerbera daisies and marguerites in a bright-red glass caddy got at the hardware store; red napkins against the background of a gray tablecloth; some black tableware. Intriguing.

Spring
For spring, lilac blossoms, snowball hydrangea, and wild dill in a hand-painted Chinese straw basket. The lacy embroidery of the linens and the pink undercloth continue the gentle theme. This is the time to bring out the majolica if you have it and to add, as a final touch, a straw hat done up with flowers and ribbons.

56

Summer

Be lavish in your use of summer's bounty. Fill an old watering can with flowers, a basket with fresh, colorful vegetables. Even for a weekend supper in the city you can finish off this country-picnic look with some gardening shears, terra cotta pots, and a gardening hat on top of a nubby-textured linen tablecloth.

Fall

Decorating with fall flowers doesn't limit you to mums. Keep an eye out for unusual flowers and dried grasses at roadsides and in the woods. Scour city farmers' markets. Here, two kinds of grapes and everlasting protea from South Africa work well with lavender tablecloth, hunter-green napkins, and green and yellow dishes.

Move some of your favorite "collectibles" to the dining table if they would enhance a theme. This Oriental porcelain figurine might lend a special touch of the Far East to a menu featuring ginger.

It helps to remember that a theme doesn't always have to be obvious; in fact, it may be noticeable only to you. But because it has helped you to plan your party more imaginatively and confidently, your guests will pick up on these touches and enjoy the party even more.

There will also be times when you just want a very pretty table, with an arrangement of flowers that echoes the colors of your china pattern or adds color along with the tablecloth and napkins. If you're working with a florist to achieve this look, it's wise to remember that even the prettiest grouping of flowers will look less than their best in those run-of-the-mill plastic floral containers that most florists use. Don't let this happen. Provide the florist with your own containers, which may range from flower vases to any number of diverse items you have in your house: a copper chafing dish, a Limoges compote, your grandmother's porcelain sugar bowl, a silver or crystal bowl, or handsome baskets. As an alternative, you could wrap the florist's plastic containers with some suitable fabric, or even burlap, and tie them around the rim with ribbon.

Now for the Flourishes

Your choice of flowers or some other decorative element depends on your budget and your preferences. Flowers, except in winter in cold climates, don't have to cost a fortune, and even in winter less·expensive varieties are available. One of the more memorable arrangements of recent memory was seen in the living room of a "camp" in the Adirondack Mountains. A huge brass jar had been filled with black-eyed Susans and sprigs of Queen Anne's lace. The effect was spectacular, and it didn't cost a penny. To stretch your budget, add a few real flowers to an arrangement of dried flowers, or artfully combine some silk or other fabric flowers with a few real ones.

More ways to stretch your flower money: Buy single flowers and put them in bud vases, one at each place setting. Or use several bud vases at the center of the table, and fill each one with a different flower in the same color. For example, you could use one white tulip, one white peony, one white rose, and one white iris. Cut the stems to different lengths, use white lacy paper or linen table mats, white napkins, and a pale-green linen tablecloth, for a springlike table. Build a whole arrangement of concentric circles of bud vases in the center of the table and fill them with a variety of flowers in different colors, their stems cut to different lengths. Place the vase with the tallest flower in the center, lowering the height with each additional circle of vases.

Incidentally, putting a large round mirror in the center of your table underneath the flowers will double the effect of the flowers.

Depending on the season, you may want to forgo flowers altogether and do a wonderful arrangement of fruit or vegetables. The key here is to think bountiful: Use a lot of whatever you've got, for maximum effect. In the fall, line a stoneware dish with magnolia leaves; then fill the dish with lots of polished apples. In summer, fill a real tomato basket with shined-up tomatoes, and make a circle of curly parsley all around the edge of the basket. Fill in the spaces between the tomatoes with more parsley or with white daisies.

Special touches are always welcome. In the fall or winter, make little cornucopias of twisted brown paper and fill them with assorted unshelled nuts. Put a cornucopia at each place setting, letting some of the nuts spill out onto the table, and place beside it a small nutcracker. People like having things to do at the table when they're not occupied with eating: It eases any gaps in the conversation.

Another idea: Instead of one menu card per table, get a small slate for each place setting and write the menu on it with chalk. Lay a piece of chalk and a small chalk eraser alongside each menu. People can scribble on their slates during dinner.

In addition to your table arrangements, special effects for your party can be achieved with garlands, trellises, and roping. How or whether you choose to use them depends on the space you want to decorate. Both can hide ugly architectural details and enhance nice ones. Suppose you're taking over several large rooms in an historic mansion. To add your own personal touch, you may want to garland the doorways—either simply with leaves or with leaves and flowers—as well as a less-than-pretty mantelpiece or even window frames that need a fresh coat of paint. Stairways look wonderful with roping looped around the banisters. A particularly effective combination is rope covered with heather, then tied with African daisies, lilacs, and tulips. Roping or trellising can be used

simply to prettify an entrance or actually to create one of some distinction. This is an especially good idea if you're using a tent, which certainly needs some dressing up before it joins the party. And this leads us to:

Tent Talk

A tent, all by itself, is merely a shelter, a guarantee that your party will go on outdoors, regardless of the weather. After choosing the tent for your party, the next challenge is to turn the tent into a beautiful party *room*. And to do this, you need some way of enclosing the space or of giving the illusion of enclosed space. As we've pointed out, people at parties like to feel close to each other in a spacial sense: It's friendlier and more festive. Trellises provide one attractive way of making a tent more roomlike. Used at the sides of the tent, they can serve as background for real or good artificial flowers or greenery, or, as we saw at the Heinz party, for posters depicting the highlights of the guest of honor's life. An alternative to trellising the perimeters of a tent is to stretch some sheer, light-colored fabric between poles along the sides of the tent. This allows light and air in yet still gives the illusion of "walls."

Incidentally, it's just as much of a challenge to make a very large and very high indoor space seem more intimate and personal. One way it's done—for instance, in the grand hall of a museum or art gallery—is by tenting each separate round table with an umbrellalike structure made of a light wooden frame that is covered with greens and

Inspiration for an arrangement of flowers often comes simply by taking a fresh look at the things in the room around you. A prized painting or lithograph, for instance, may suggest highlighting a detail from the artist's canvas. At left is a section of a dramatic and oversize grouping of night-blooming water lilies, heliconia, ginger, and honeysuckle vine. Their vibrant colors and angular shapes make a stunning foil for the six-foot-tall abstract painting hanging on the wall behind the flowers. Anything less assertive would look out of place. In addition to highlighting the owner's magnificent collection of modern art, the flowers resolve the need to make the imposing space of a contemporary, two-story-high living room more personal.

twined with flowers. Then each table seems as though it has its own little roof, under which the diners are in their own private world within the larger universe of the party.

Outdoors, in a tent, or indoors, in your home, lighting is a major consideration. Unfortunately, it's one that too few party givers understand or even consider. So let's consider it here.

A tent may be a practical safeguard against inclement weather, but the very sight of one tells you it's really there to herald a happy event. They come in every conceivable color, shape, and size, to fit any requirement, but most tents indicate a wedding.

be depressing. Lighting all through your house or party location should be soft and pretty and should make your guests feel comfortable and at their most attractive. Even the kitchen and the powder room should have soft lighting; otherwise the effect of going into them from other rooms can be like that of stepping out of a moviehouse on a bright afternoon—startling. Downlighting of any kind, except for a tiny spotlight in the ceiling directly over the center of a dining table, should be on dimmers. The most interesting lighting will come from uplighting; that is, light that beams up from the floor or near the floor.

For lighting a big party in a large setting, you may want to go to a theatrical-lighting-supply store, such as Times Square Lighting, in New York City, and rent Par cans. These holders can be fitted with high-intensity spot or flood bulbs, and they're adjustable, so you can focus the light exactly where you want it. They come equipped with wall brackets, table bases, or pipe or spring clamps, so you can rest them on the floor, attach them to wall moldings, or even place them on plant containers. Light that filters up through the leaves of potted palms makes wonderfully dramatic shadows on the ceiling. (Caution: These bulbs get very hot, so they should never be aimed directly at foliage or flammable containers.) You can also get gels (colored plastic disks that fit over the bulbs) that will soften the lights to a luminous warm pink or amber. (Don't use blue unless you want to create a chilly look, appropriate for a Christmas tree covered with "snow" or an ice-sculpture centerpiece on a buffet table.)

For a smaller party at home, a trip to your hardware store should yield the kind of small, clamp-on industrial fixtures that hold pin lights (smaller versions of spotlights). These are effective attached to plant containers or placed beside or behind a grouping of plants for dramatic shadows.

David Tiller, of Bullard's, in Dallas, set the mood for an adult birthday party with a centerpiece of boxes covered with colorful paper and made to look like giant building blocks, and then he stacked them at crazy angles.

Lighting

More than any other element, lighting creates the mood of a party. When you think about lighting, keep in mind two things: making your guests look their best and creating drama. Too much light drains color from people's faces and causes harsh shadows, creates a feeling of tension rather than of relaxation. Yet, insufficient light can

This stunning holiday treatment for the stairs of a contemporary Colonial-style home is made up of juniper roping, holly, pink azaleas and velvet ribbon, Granny Smith apples, kumquats, and oranges. Fitting symbols of hospitality, the ornamental pineapples are crowning touches on the railings.

For dining tables: candles, candles, and more candles. Candles by themselves make a wonderful centerpiece, especially a whole grouping of candles of varying widths and heights in the center of the table. (But no scented candles except in the bathrooms, please.) Or you can use a marvelous ornate candelabrum, or a pair of candelabra, with tall tapers. White candles used to be *de rigueur* for dinner parties. Now any color you like is fine; they all give off the same soft, yellow light. Candles and flower centerpieces should be of compatible heights: A tall group of flowers needs eight-inch candles; lower arrangements can take shorter candles or a ring of votive candles in clear glass holders. Votive-candle holders can be wrapped with galax leaves and tied with a bit of straw or ribbon. Apples and artichokes, cored, make unusual holders for votive candles.

Use mini shelf lights (available through mail order) to highlight bookshelves and play up pretty bibelots in curio cabinets; this is an inexpensive way to create interesting illumination without installing more costly ceiling lighting.

Illuminating the outdoors and any large open space such as a tent calls for more ingenuity than wattage. Here, an electrician was brought in to provide a temporary generator to supply the lighting for more than four hundred guests.

Party lighting at its best makes your guests look and feel great. It also creates fantasy, as in this elegant scene where pin lights, uplighting, dimmers, camoflaged lighting, candles, and every other trick of the party designer's trade come out of the hat.

Outdoors, too, more lighting, rather than less, is the rule. The great outdoors, even if it's only a backyard, absorbs light the way a sponge does water, so plan on more lighting (floodlights, mainly) for your trees and garden. Work with an electrician if you're planning a major lighting job, so that on the night of the party you don't blow out the lights in your house when the lights go on outside. Of course, candles (in hurricane lamps or some other kind of sheltering cover) are as lovely outside as in, but candles alone can't provide your lighting outdoors, even on a porch or patio. Augment the candlelight there with uplighting from reflector bulbs or pinlights in clamp-on fixtures (on porch railings) or in fixtures with flat bases that can rest on the floor.

Recently those strings of small white Christmas-tree lights have come into popular use to outline branches of trees. A bit of this is quite effective, but it's often overdone. It's best to make a feature out of one or two trees, then floodlight the rest. Driveways or garden paths can be outlined with light as well. Place candles in paper bags that have been waxed, then filled halfway with sand.

Entertainment

With the essentials taken care of, it's time to think about whether or not you want some kind of entertainment at your party. Of course, for many of us, the party itself is entertainment, especially if the guest list has been carefully arranged so that there are plenty of live wires and good conversationalists to spark the evening. But you may decide that the task of amusing one another shouldn't be borne solely by your guests. In that case, you can have a great deal of fun deciding exactly what kind of outside entertainment you would like to bring in. The choice is enormous, even in small towns. You'll probably find plenty of talent right there, or, if you want something extra special, big-city performers will travel (for a fee). Music schools are a good place to find musicians who can play for your party. Young musicians love to play at parties: The pay is good and the atmosphere pleasant. You may want a single musician—a pianist, violinist, or harpist—or a trio. At a big party, one of the best ways of encouraging guests to leave the rooms where they are

Home movies on a giant video screen provide larger-than-life entertainment for a gala evening in celebration of a seventieth birthday. At a large reunion, old and young are treated to a spritely taste of family history (granddaddy doing a cake walk in his teens?) along with a gourmet dinner.

A novel alternative to candles for a buffet table is the type of sculptured neon lighting you see in storefront windows. Here, a neon cactus looks right at home with an arrangement of plants indigenous to the Southwest, as well as more conventional flowers such as alium, rubrum lily, gerbera daisies, and liatris.

having cocktails and to move into the dining room is to send a flutist, or even a bagpipe player, into the rooms, to act as a modern Pied Piper to summon guests in to dinner.

You may decide to plan your whole party around the music and give a musicale. The musical part of the evening can occur first or after a meal, which may be a sit-down

clowns, etc. There are also people who will videotape your party and present you with an edited or unedited version (the edited version costs more and includes the addition of background music, titles, and subtitles). Of course, there are dance bands and country-and-western bands for hire as well. Again, think small-town talent when yours is a small budget, and *audition* the group before you hire them. The prices of big-time bands, though not stratospheric, are high.

In cities, especially New York, the streets are alive with entertainers, many of whom love to do parties. Break dancers and pop dancers (pop is the new son of break dancing) can be found this way, as can some very good musicians.

Music adds to the gaiety of any social gathering. Whether the party theme is "south of the border" or "Scottish folk dancing," it is easy to find talented musicians eager to play for you, even in small towns.

dinner or a buffet, or simply cheese and wine, or a buffet of desserts after the music.

At Christmas, you may want to hire some professional singers to give a short performance of carols. Singers should be considered performers and not "background music." Trying to use carolers as background music, by stationing them in a hallway where people pass through to get to the dining room, is rude to the singers—who are singing their hearts out while no one is listening—and can be embarrassing to your guests (especially those who appreciate good singing voices). Entertainment should be considered just that—a featured attraction. Unlike the cocktail pianist, the jazz pianist is meant to be listened to, and might come in after dinner for a short recital.

Other available entertainment: people who play hand bells or wine glasses (filled to different heights with water), handwriting experts, sand readers, palm readers, mimes, trained animals with their trainers, belly dancers,

With your party plan worked out in detail, you are now well on your way. But first a note about the actual doing of it. If you don't want to find yourself tearing your hair at the last minute, remind yourself daily of two things: 1) Almost everything will take longer than you anticipate, so allow a cushion for each item on your daily list. 2) Be prepared to make adjustments as you go along; there will be times when the exact product you want is not available. Even professional party planners and cooks have to—and frequently do—make changes midstream.

This French lettuce basket was used to combine kale and dill with daisies and yellow lilies—an effortless arrangement that would be charming outdoors or in.

For anyone needing directions to a party, a visual signpost is a thoughtful gesture. A floral welcome sign is a particularly nice touch: It assures guests that they are expected and that you are looking forward to their company. A lovely bouquet of yellow lilies with a trail of English ivy hangs over the iron balustrade leading up to an old house in Charleston, South Carolina.

Finishing Touches

This means reviewing your preparations and seeing if you've left out anything that's important for the comfort of your guests. Are there guest towels in the bathrooms? Is the lighting soft and flattering? Have you remembered to put out fresh soaps and nosegays of sweet, scented flowers?

Are you sure the directions to your house are clear? You may want to augment your written or oral instructions to your guests with visual aids. One way to do this, if the party is during the day, is to tie brightly colored bandannas around trees or signposts along the way and to alert people to look for these. Or, for an even more original method, hire mimes or clowns to stand at intervals along the road pointing the way or holding signs with arrows.

Are the help alerted as to the time you want them to appear?

Do you have plenty of ice? Is the liquor store open late that night, in case the supply gets low?

Are you ready to have a good time at your own party? Then you will, and so will your guests.

The Party's Over

Or, at any rate, it's time for it to be over. The most diplomatic way of indicating that it's time for remaining guests to leave is to alert a friend or two, before the party, to make leaving noises at the end of the evening, even to offer to drop home any lingering guests who can't take a hint. It's also nice to invite a few special friends to stay on for a party post-mortem after the rest of the guests

Finishing touches for a party include giving thought to the guests' needs. Have extra hangers on hand, or rent a coat rack for a spare room. Put out special hand towels and fragrant soap in the bathroom. Have Kleenex and a spare comb and brush handy. Clear the medicine cabinet of unnecessary clutter, leaving miscellaneous niceties on the shelves such as aspirin, Band-Aids, mouthwash, and the like. Flowers in the powder room are appreciated. Here, a mirrored container reflected in the bathroom mirror doubles the impact of a loose arrangement of pink tulips, heather, and protea.

have left. Taking your shoes off and having a nightcap with a few chums is a cozy way of coming down from a party high. After all, you've worked on this evening for some time and it's easy to feel a little let down if the door closes and everyone's gone all at once.

If this has not been a catered party, arrange ahead of time to have someone come in the next day—a cleaning service or your regular weekly cleaning help—to put the house back in order. This is a special treat you owe yourself. After all, the easier you make it for yourself, the more often you'll want to entertain.

Don't wait too long to add up the real expenses of the party versus your estimated party budget. A day or two after the party is a good time to record the actual figures in your party notebook, a great help when planning your next party, and a real eye opener when you compare today's party prices with those of previous years.

Remember, the more you entertain, the more party-perfect—and relaxed—you will become.

PART THREE

Fabulous Food

Party Countdown

*O*rganizing a party may seem a cinch. Just decide on a date, a guest list, a budget, and an outline for a menu. After that, it's merely a question of following through, right? Well, yes and no. Although the beginning stages of party planning are fun and uncomplicated, that first vision of a dazzling, perfect event can be quickly sabotaged by any one of a number of unforeseen, last-minute problems. All of us are familiar with these mini-catastrophies: The grocery store leaves the strawberries out of your order; you forget to put the roast in the oven; the mousse won't jell; and the doorbell rings before you've had a chance to change your clothes or even brush your hair.

Is there any way around these unanticipated disasters? Party experts around the country agree that hard work alone is not enough to bring order to the countless details that go into orchestrating a smoothly run event. For any party, they all say, planning and keeping lists are vitally important. So are flexible schedules.

But how do you translate that expert advice into a plan that works? The answer, perhaps, is to avoid the two most common mistakes in party giving: *underestimating* the amount of time needed to bring all the elements together and *overextending* yourself with goals too ambitious to be reached.

So, begin with a practical schedule that will take you every step of the way, from a Day One master plan, three weeks in advance, through the last half hour before the guests arrive, concluding with the clearing of the last few dessert plates and coffee cups.

As suggested earlier, start a party notebook. Make it your constant companion, jotting down ideas as they oc-cur to you. This will help you organize yourself, making you see exactly where you are running ahead of or behind schedule. But always keep in mind as you are making your lists that nothing will work if you don't have the hours or the help to implement your plans. As you begin writing down your menu, for instance, it might seem at first to be a lovely idea to have both hot and cold hors-d'oeuvres. But wait a minute. How practical will that be when your oven is crammed with the roast that you're planning to serve as a main course? Also, you might ask yourself which is more important—dazzling your guests with your non-stop culinary triumphs or joining your guests in the fun.

Begin planning with your own fun in mind. Divide your party notebook into several sections, allowing a few blank pages for each. Following is a list of suggested head-ings for each section:

- guest list
- party telephone directory
- menu and rough preparation time
- utensils and equipment
- liquor, wines, and bartending arrangements
- shopping list
- final week's day-to-day cooking schedule

Since your party will begin with the invitations you send, make this the first list in your notebook. Write down all the names of the people you've invited and their tele-phone numbers. As the RSVPs come in, check them off, making follow-up calls to those you haven't heard from.

The next entry in your notebook should be a handy list of all the names and telephone numbers of the people who will be assisting you with the party: liquor store, bartender, grocery store (for last-minute orders), florist, cook, waitress, rental company, ice supplier, babysitter, and, yes, even the kennels if your rambunctious puppy is being banished for the evening. If you're giving a really big party, it might be useful to include the numbers for a taxi service, the car parkers, the fire department, the hospital, and the police.

Begin working on your menu right away. Most people start with the main course, building around a dish they feel confident about. As you roughly pencil in everything from appetizers to dessert, keep in mind the various colors and textures of everything as well as the season of the year and the availability of fresh fruits and vegetables. Next, pencil in the approximate cooking times for each item on your menu and the cooking utensils you'll need for each. Does everything you've chosen require day-of-the-party preparation? If so, change the menu immediately to include food that can be prepared well in advance and set aside, either refrigerated or frozen. Will your stove or oven or refrigerator accommodate all the food you've chosen? Will your oven or burners be overloaded at the last minute? How about your supply of pots and pans, casseroles and baking dishes? The last thing you'll want is to have to rush out to the hardware store the day of the party to buy a casserole dish you'll never use again!

Now that you've chosen your menu, it's time to turn your attention to the wine and other assorted drinks you'll be serving. If you're planning a big party, you should have lined up the caterer and bartender before you even invited the first guest. If that's the case, they can help you. Just tell any experienced bartender how many guests you're expecting and he or she will be able to estimate accurately how much liquor you'll need for the cocktail hour. It's better to err on the generous side; unopened bottles are returnable.

Next, find the spot where you plan to set up the bar, remembering that at most parties it tends to be the most congested place of all. Choose an area where there will be enough space for the traffic to flow easily. Next, check your bar equipment. Do you have a couple of good-sized pitchers, a container large enough for plenty of ice, a jigger, a long spoon, a paring knife for slicing lemons and limes, a small wooden cutting board, and a corkscrew opener for wine drinkers? These are among the essential tools that all bartenders need.

The wines you serve at dinner will, of course, be determined by your menu. Enlist the advice of a reliable wine merchant if you don't have a precise idea of what might complement the foods you have planned. If your menu dictates white wine or champagne, consider how you plan to cool the bottles. Since your refrigerator will probably be full, rent or borrow a galvanized or plastic ice tub (an empty bathtub filled with ice would serve the purpose). Whatever dinner wines you serve, however, remember that an astonishing difference in quality exists even among vintage wines. No matter what price range you choose, do some prior wine tasting. A good meal deserves a good wine: Buy the best you can to fit the occasion.

Having ordered your liquor and wine, go back for another look at your menu. In your party notebook, make a shopping list of all the ingredients you'll need. Divide the list into four subheadings: 1) staples you can order in advance; 2) fresh items needed; 3) ingredients you already have on hand (and be sure that such oft-overlooked items as sugar, salt, and flour aren't running low); and 4) kitchen staples such as plastic or aluminum wrap, paper towels, dishwasher detergent.

Next, make a detailed list of all the equipment you'll need. Start with the cooking utensils. Is everything scoured and ready for use? Nothing can be quite as annoying as reaching into the oven to find the broiler pan laden with burnt-on grease! In matching your pots and pans to the specific recipes you've chosen, you may find that you'll have to borrow a few things from friends. Count your glasses, dinner plates, and flatware, too. Then borrow or rent those extras.

If you've decided to hire a caterer, either telephone him now or, better still, arrange a time when he can come over to look at your kitchen facilities. He should be able to give you excellent professional advice about what you'll need for twenty, fifty, or a hundred guests, and you'll have a chance to let him see your personal style. And that's important. After all, even if your party is totally catered, it must reflect you. If the food presentation is too "staged," it will seem as if the party were taking place in

some hotel. The presentation should make use of at least some of your silver, china, and linen, and should represent your personal taste in food and decor, or else you could feel like a stranger in your own home.

The final list in your party notebook should be a detailed, day-by-day breakdown of everything that must be done during the final week before the party. This should include flower arranging, shopping, cleaning your house, making a seating list, writing place cards, and, above all, cooking.

How much of the meal can be done ahead of time? The well-known author and culinary authority, Sallie Y. Williams, estimates that 80 percent of all food preparation is advance work, such as shopping, peeling, chopping, grating, whipping, and refrigerating; 10 percent consists of such final touches as decorating and garnishing; the final

10 percent, actual cooking time. Moreover, her approach makes kitchen work not only easier and quicker but much less prone to calamity. For each recipe, she uses a cookie sheet on which she lines up her premeasured ingredients in small bowls and cups. Having everything she needs within a hand's reach is not only time-saving but keeps the kitchen neat and organized.

Figure out what can be prepared in advance—perhaps the cold chocolate mousse you're serving for dessert or the cucumber soup or the chopped onions you'll sauté later. Begin cleaning out your refrigerator, to make room for the party food. Meanwhile, in a leisurely way, start making your seating chart, cleaning your house, polishing the silver, and writing out place cards, allotting one or two of these chores to each of the earlier days in the week.

The day before the party is countdown time. Chances

are that your party notebook wil be crammed with things to do because today will be your busiest day of all. Today, much of your menu can be fully assembled and prepared except for the final heating, and you can set your table and do most of your flower arranging. Be sure also to check in with the people who will be assisting you. Do you know exactly what time the bartender and waitress plan to arrive? Does the liquor merchant know that he's supposed to include several bags of ice with your order? If you're not sure of some of these things, find out now.

The day of the big event, in fact, should be the least busy day in your party notebook. Instead of frantically rushing around, totally exhausting yourself, you should wake up today to see your dinner table already set, your food almost totally prepared, your house sparkling with flowers, your silver and crystal gleaming. Chances are, however, that the phone will start ringing early and never stop. It may be a guest calling to say she's in bed with the flu, which will mean that you must quickly rejuggle the seating arrangement. Or it might be the liquor store again, asking you to have a check ready when they make their afternoon delivery. The doorbell might ring with a surprise package, an azalea plant from one of the guests. How was the thoughtful sender of that plant to know that your living room features a color plan of hot reds and oranges, leaving you nonplussed about where to put the pink plant?

Indeed, a thousand and one unexpected things can happen on the day of the party. So leave your calender open, and, above all, prepare to be flexible. After you've finished with all but the latest of preparations, try to relax and pamper yourself. If you've hired help to come in and take over from you during the late afternoon, give them final instructions and tell them to take all phone messages. Then, take a long, soothing bath, stretch out on your bed for a while, and, later, take your time getting dressed. Okay? Now, all alone, wander through the stage setting you've created. Turn down the electric lights, light the candles, and bask in the pleasure of a Beautiful Party.

A Cook's Miscellany

Most cooks clip miscellaneous scraps of useful culinary hints, techniques, shortcuts, substitutes, charts, and the like for easy reference. The problem is that too often these are hard to find when needed. Here is a small collection of such miscellany, arranged alphabetically. Also included are a few basic recipes not spelled out in the pages that follow. Some of the menus have listings that are intentionally vague. Assorted Tea Sandwiches, for example, are limitless in their combination, cuts, textures, and designs. We leave those broad decisions to the reader, since so much depends on time, availability, and budget.

Bouquet Garni

This bouquet of herbs is used to flavor soups, stews, sauces, stocks, and braised meat and vegetables. Bay leaf and sprigs of parsley and thyme are usually tied to a rib of celery or in a piece of leek with kitchen twine. The bundle is removed after the dish is cooked. If using dried or loose herbs, tie them in a piece of clean cheesecloth. Onion, cloves, garlic, and rosemary may be added to the bouquet.

Canapés

Canapés are thin slices of bread or toast spread with any variety of meats, vegetables, cheeses, or fish, but are often used interchangeably with hors-d'oeuvres. To make canapés, trim crust from thin slices of plain white or dark bread and cut each slice into rounds or triangles. Sauté in clarified butter until golden brown, or toast in a 250° oven until dried out. Bread may also be used fresh. For hot canapés, top with desired filling (crab and mayonnaise, ham and mayonnaise, chopped chicken livers, etc.), sprinkle with grated cheese, heat to bubbling under broiler, and serve promptly. If fresh bread is preferred, follow directions for tea sandwiches, using such toppings as red and black caviar with chopped white onions, anchovy and cheese, or salmon and cream cheese.

Herbs and Spices

Whether fresh-grown or store-bought, a good array of herbs and spices should be kept on hand. Keep fresh herbs refrigerated, and don't wash them until ready to use. If you buy your herbs, look for large leaves with a strong perfume. Crush them in the palm of your hand or with a mortar and pestle just before adding to a dish, to release additional flavor. When substituting dried for fresh, figure on one teaspoon dried herbs for one tablespoon fresh. Often-used herbs: basil, bay leaf, chives, coriander, dill, mint, parsley, rosemary, sage, tarragon, and thyme. Dried herbs lose their potency quickly, so buy in small amounts or replace frequently. Store in a cool, dark place. For spices, it's preferable to buy them whole and grind them as you use them. Often-used spices: allspice, caraway seeds, cloves, cinnamon, ginger, mace, nutmeg, and peppercorns. As with dried herbs, keep ground spices away from heat and light.

Mayonnaise

Makes 2½ cups

3 egg yolks, at room temperature
1 tablespoon lemon juice
1 teaspoon dry mustard
Salt and pepper
1 cup vegetable oil
1 cup olive oil

Place yolks in the container of a food processor or blender fitted with a steel blade. Process for 60 seconds. Stop machine and add lemon juice, mustard, and salt and pepper to taste. Process with 2 short pulses. Combine oils in large container. With machine running, add oil by drops until mixture begins to thicken. Add remaining oil in a slow, steady stream and mix until smooth. Cover tightly and refrigerate up to 1 week.

Note: *For different accents, try adding any one of the following: fresh, minced green herbs (tarragon, basil, dill, chervil, chives, parsley, oregano); chopped cooked spinach; tomato puree; crushed garlic; crushed capers; chopped cornichons; chopped anchovies; or Dijon or honey mustard.*

Oils

Oils vary greatly in quality, taste, and price. Some are so refined that they are nearly tasteless and odorless. Others, usually the more expensive, are pure, unrefined oils, which really enhance food flavor. Finding the ones you like will take a bit of experimentation. Store in a cool, dark place and in hot weather buy them in small quantities so that they're used before turning rancid.

Olive Oils. These are produced mainly in Italy, France, Greece, and Spain. Italian olive oils generally have a pronounced olive flavor. French olive oils tend to be lighter and fruitier. The finest grade is extra-virgin olive oil, made from the first pressing of the olives. It is best used in salads, marinades, and over hot vegetables. Virgin and pure or fine olive oil denote second and third pressings of the olive and its crushed pit.

Vegetable oils (corn, cottonseed, safflower, sunflower, soybean, peanut). Because these lack flavor and are relatively inexpensive, they are best used for deep-frying and sautéing and in mayonnaise and marinades. Peanut oil is especially good for frying since it can be heated to high temperatures without burning or darkening.

Nut oils (almond, hazelnut, walnut). These aromatic oils are great in salad dressings or tossed with hot vegetables. Use hazelnut oil to grease cake and cookie pans.

Sesame oils. These vary from the richer, thicker oils from China and Japan to the lighter, less aromatic oils of the Middle East. A few drops go a long way, so this oil can be used in combination with milder oils. Best used for cooking, in condiments, or in salad dressings.

Flavored oils. These include herb-flavored and spiced oils and are easily made at home with herbs or spices from your garden or store. Use in salad dressings and marinades or over pasta dishes.

Puff Shells (Pâté a Choux)

Makes 36–40 small puffs

1 cup water
6 tablespoons butter
1 teaspoon salt
⅛ teaspoon pepper
Pinch of nutmeg
1 cup sifted all-purpose flour
4 large eggs

In a saucepan bring water, butter, and seasonings to a boil. Remove from heat and add flour all at once. Beat with a wooden spatula to blend. Return to heat and beat over moderate heat until mixture forms a mass and leaves a film on bottom of pan, about 1 or 2 minutes. Remove from heat and beat in eggs one at a time (third and fourth eggs will take longer to incorporate). Beat until dough is smooth.

Preheat oven to 425°.

While still warm, put paste in a pastry bag and squeeze onto greased baking sheets. Make circular mounds about 1 inch in diameter and ½ inch high. Space about 2 inches apart. Dab with beaten egg, making sure that egg doesn't drip onto baking sheet (this prevents puff from rising). Bake for 20 minutes or until puffs are golden brown and firm and crusty. Do not open oven door during first half of baking time. Remove from oven and pierce bottoms with the point of a knife to release steam. Or, cut in half. Set upside down on baking sheet and set in turned-off oven with door ajar for 10 minutes. Cool on rack completely before using or storing. Puffs may be sealed in plastic and frozen.

Fillings: Mornay sauce, crab and mayonnaise, curried chicken or turkey, chopped ham in béchamel sauce.

Plain Tart Crust (Pâté Brisée)

Makes two 9-inch or 24 tartlets

2 cups all-purpose flour
½ teaspoon salt
1 stick unsalted butter, chilled and cut in bits
4 tablespoons margarine
5 tablespoons cold water

Place flour, salt, and butter in food processor. Process 15 seconds or until mixture resembles coarse meal. With processor running, add water by drops until dough forms a ball, about 15 seconds. Dough should be pliable but not damp or sticky. Wrap in plastic and refrigerate one hour before using. Dough may be kept refrigerated up to 3 days or wrapped tightly and frozen.

To make tart shells, roll out chilled dough to less than ⅛-inch thickness on a lightly floured board. Fit into tart pans and trim excess dough. Prick bottom of pastry shell with a fork. Line with buttered foil and fill with dry beans or spare tart pans, to prevent shrinkage and puffing of pastry during baking. Chill until ready to bake (up to one day). Preheat oven to 375° and bake tarts on a baking sheet for 7 to 8 minutes or until pastry holds its own shape. Remove foil and beans and prick tart shell again. Return to oven for 2 to 3 minutes to dry out. Remove and cool on racks. Place a filling in center of shell, top with a pinch of grated cheese, and put on baking sheet in a 400° oven. Bake 5 minutes or until filling is set. Serve hot or at room temperature, depending on filling. Tart shells may be baked completely, cooled, and then frozen for future use.

Suggested fillings: Leek and ham quiche; plain cheese quiche; duxelles and chopped ham; crab and mayonnaise; onion confetti.

Note: *To make a sweet tart crust for desserts, add two tablespoons sugar to the flour before making the dough.*

Puff Pastry

Makes 2 pounds pastry

1 pound unsalted butter
1 pound all-purpose flour
1 cup cold water
1 teaspoon salt

In the container of a blender or food processor, blend the butter with ½ cup flour. Form butter into a flat square, wrap in waxed paper, and chill several minutes. Process remaining flour with water and salt until the dough forms a ball. If necessary, add a few more drops of water so that dough holds together. Form dough into a flat square, wrap, and chill 15 minutes.

On a lightly floured surface, roll the dough into a 6 × 12-inch rectangle. Place butter squarely in center of dough and fold over dough to encase the butter. If necessary, chill package until butter and flour are nearly the same temperature. Place seam side down and roll into a rectangle, ⅜ inch thick. Fold in thirds, as you would a business letter. This completes the first "turn." (Lift and turn dough occasionally to make sure it doesn't stick to surface. Use as little flour as possible for rolling, and brush off any excess before folding.) Position dough so that long side with open flap is to your right, and roll out again. Fold into thirds again to complete the second turn. Wrap and chill one hour. Repeat process, making two "turns" with dough. Dough should be smooth and silky, with no visible lumps of butter. Wrap and chill 1 hour or overnight. Give the dough another two turns, to make six turns in all. Wrap and chill for at least 1 hour before using. Dough will keep 3 to 4 days in refrigerator or for months in the freezer.

Rice

Long-grain rice

Serves 4

2 cups water
1 cup long-grain rice
1 teaspoon salt
1 tablespoon butter

Place all ingredients in a large saucepan and cover tightly. Bring to a boil, reduce heat, and stir with a fork. Cover again and simmer 12 to 15 minutes, until rice is tender and all liquid is absorbed. Check tenderness by tasting a grain. Fluff before serving.

Brown rice

2½ cups water
1 cup brown rice
1 teaspoon salt

Follow same procedure as with long-grain rice, but simmer brown rice for 45 minutes.

Wild rice

2 cups water
1 cup wild rice
1 teaspoon salt
3 tablespoons butter

Wash rice well and drain thoroughly. Bring water to a boil in a saucepan. Stir in rice and salt. Reduce heat, cover, and simmer 40 to 50 minutes, until rice is tender and all liquid is absorbed. Toss butter in and blend with a fork till melted.

Note: *Rice may be prepared hours in advance, then covered and refrigerated. To reheat, steam until hot or sauté briefly in butter.*

Salad Greens

Use a single type or create contrasts of color, taste, and texture using a variety of salad greens: Boston, bibb, chicory, endive, escarole, iceberg, red, green, romaine, arrugula, watercress, spinach, radicchio, and sorrel. For tossed salads, allow one large handful of salad per person. Rinse greens in cold water, separating leaves to remove all sand and dirt. Discard wilted or discolored leaves. Shake off excess water and allow lettuce to dry, or spin dry in a salad dryer; salad dressings won't cling to wet leaves. Tear into small pieces or wrap leaves in cloth or paper towel and refrigerate from 12 to 24 hours. Toss with dressing just before serving, to avoid soggy greens. For unusual accents, try adding grated carrots or zucchini, shredded meats or seafood, or nuts.

Tea Sandwiches

Tea sandwiches can add a touch of sophistication to any tea or cocktail party. Certain fillings are traditional, but don't hesitate to experiment with creative flavor combinations. Sandwiches should be made as close to serving time as possible but will hold several hours if kept cool and wrapped in damp cloth. Butter or mayonnaise is used to prevent the bread from drying out and to prevent it from becoming soggy from juicy fillings. To make the sandwiches, trim crusts from thinly sliced bread and spread slices with softened butter or mayonnaise. Cut into rounds, squares, or triangles, according to shape of filling. Arrange filling on one slice and top with another slice.

Note: *For added variety, try flavored butters and mayonnaise.*

Vinegars

As with oils, there's a vast array of vinegars of different flavors, and these vary greatly in price.

Distilled vinegars. These are made by distilling alcohol and are best used for pickling.

Wine vinegars (red and white, sherry, champagne, balsamic). These are generally the most costly, but are worth the price. Use in vinaigrettes, marinades, and sauces.

Cider vinegars. Can range from bland supermarket brands to very good vinegars made from whole apples. Use for general cooking, pickling, and preserving and in potato salad or cole slaw.

Herb and fruit vinegars. Both are easy to make at home with fresh fruits and herbs and are best used in salad dressings and marinades.

Vinaigrette

Makes 1⅓ cups

⅓ cup vinegar
½ teaspoon dry or Dijon mustard
1 cup olive or vegetable oil
Salt and freshly ground pepper

Beat vinegar and mustard together. Slowly whisk in oil until fully incorporated. Season to taste. Use immediately or refrigerate in a jar.

Note: *For variation, add any one of the following: fresh, chopped herbs; minced anchovies; crushed garlic; lemon juice; honey mustard; minced shallot.*

Average Single Serving of Common Foods	
meat, poultry, fish	4 ounces = ¼ pound
vegetables, fruits	½ cup
ice cream, desserts	½ cup
pies	⅐ of a 9 inch
cakes	2-inch wedge

QUANTITIES FOR CROWDS	20	50	100
HORS-D'OEUVRES			
Cheeses...............................	2–4 lbs.	5–7 lbs.	14–16 lbs.
Chips..................................	3 bags	5 bags	10 bags
Crackers	1 lb.	2 lbs.	4 lbs.
Dips...................................	3 cups	5 cups	10 cups
Finger foods.........................	10–13 doz.	34 doz.	68–70 doz.
Nuts	1 lb.	2½ lbs.	4 lbs.
SOUPS...............................	6 qts.	12 qts.	24 qts.
MAIN COURSE			
Ground meats	5 lbs.	12 lbs.	25 lbs.
Cold cuts	5 lbs.	12 lbs.	25 lbs.
Meat (Boneless).....................	5 lbs.	12 lbs.	25 lbs.
Poultry	10 lbs.	25 lbs.	50 lbs.
Fish (Fillets).........................	5 lbs.	12 lbs.	25 lbs.
ACCOMPANIMENTS			
Pasta	1 lb.	2½ lbs.	5–6 lbs.
Potatoes	5 lbs.	12–14 lbs.	25 lbs.
Rice....................................	5 cups	12 cups	24 cups
Tossed salad	3 qts.	8 qts.	16–20 qts.
Vegetables	5 lbs.	12 lbs.	25 lbs.
BREADS			
Loaves.................................	2½ lbs.	4 lbs.	8 lbs.
Rolls...................................	2½ doz.	6–8 doz.	14 doz.
DESSERTS			
Cakes..................................	2	4–5	8–10
Cookies...............................	5 doz.	12 doz.	20–24 doz.
Ice cream	1 gal.	2 gal.	4 gal.
Pies	3	5–6	10
Whipped cream for topping	1 pt.	2½ pts.	4 pts.
MISCELLANEOUS			
Butter	½ lb.	1 lb.	2 lbs.
Coffee (⅓ decaffeinated, ⅔ regular)	¾ lb.	1½ lbs.	3 lbs.
Cream for coffee	2 cups	4 cups	8 cups
Sugar..................................	1 cup	2 cups	4 cups
Ice cubes for cocktails.............	20–25 lbs.	50–60 lbs.	100–125 lbs.

EQUIVALENTS AND SUBSTITUTIONS

almonds, shelled	¼ pound = 1 cup
apples, raw	1 pound or 3 medium = 3 cups, pared and sliced
asparagus	1 pound = 15–25 stalks
baking powder	1 teaspoon = ¼ teaspoon baking soda
beans, fresh green	3 pounds = 4 cups
beans, dried	1 pound = 6 cups, cooked
bread	1 pound = 12–16 slices
butter	1 stick = ½ cup = ¼ pound = 8 tablespoons
cabbage, raw	1 pound = 4 cups, shredded
candied fruits or peels	½ pound = 1¼ cups
cheese, grated	¼ pound = 1 cup
chocolate	1 square = 1 ounce = 1 tablespoon, melted = 4 tablespoons, grated = 3 tablespoons cocoa plus 1 tablespoon butter
chicken, drawn weight	4 pounds = 4 cups, diced
coffee	1 pound = 80 tablespoons or 40 cups
cornstarch	1 tablespoon = 2 tablespoons flour
crabmeat	1 pound = 2 cups
cream, heavy	1 cup = 2 cups, whipped
flour, all purpose	1 pound = 4 cups = 1 ounce = 4 tablespoons
garlic	1 clove = ⅛ teaspoon garlic powder
gelatin	1 envelope = 1 tablespoon = ¼ ounce
herbs, fresh	1 tablespoon = 1 teaspoon, dried
lard	½ pound = 1 cup
lemon	1 = 2–3 tablespoons juice = 2 teaspoons grated rind
macaroni, uncooked	¼ pound = 1 cup, dry = 2¼ cups, cooked
meat, cooked, diced	1 cup = 5 ounces, 1 pound = 3 cups
meat, ground	1 pound = 2 cups

mushrooms, fresh, sliced	1 pound = 5 cups
nut meats, chopped	1 pound = 4 cups
orange	1 = 6–8 tablespoons juice = ⅓ cup = 6 portions
rice, uncooked	1 cup = 3 cups, cooked, 1 pound = 1½ cups, uncooked = 8 cups, cooked
salt	1 ounce = 1½ teaspoons
shrimp, cooked	1 pound = 2 cups
spaghetti	1 pound = 10 cups, cooked
spinach	1¼ pounds = 1 cup, cooked
sugar, granulated	1 pound = 2¼ cups, 8 ounces = 1 cup
tea	1 pound = 120 cups
tomatoes, fresh, whole	1 pound = 4 tomatoes = 1 cup, cooked, chopped
vegetables, raw, chopped	½ pound = 1 cup

STANDARD WEIGHTS AND MEASURES

dash / 8 drops
1 teaspoon / 60 drops
1 tablespoon / 3 teaspoons
1 pony / ½ fluid ounce
1 ounce / 2 tablespoons
1 jigger / 3 tablespoons = 1½ fluid ounces
¼ cup / 4 tablespoons

⅓ cup / 5½ tablespoons
1 pint / 2 cups
1 pound / 16 ounces
1 quart / 2 pints
1 gallon / 4 quarts
1 peck / 8 quarts
1 bushel / 4 pecks

1 cup / 16 tablespoons = 8 fluid ounces = ½ pint

MENU CONTENTS

Black-tie, Seated Dinner

Curiously, giving a formal dinner party often requires less rather than more work than other modes of entertaining. Think about it. At more casual gatherings you are free to go back and forth from the kitchen to finish up the last-minute cooking. Timing isn't as crucial. At a buffet, who'll notice that you forgot to put out the rolls warmed in the oven if there aren't butter plates out on the table?

Whether it's black tie for six or sixty, a seated dinner does require you to be completely there for your guests. Nothing is more disconcerting than a distracted, flustered hostess who unwittingly gives the impression the visitors are an intrusion.

The key is in the planning and in keeping everything ridiculously simple, as was demonstrated by an elegant dinner for sixty, prepared by one of Chicago's leading caterers, Patrick Collins. It was created for a woman who wanted to celebrate her sixtieth wedding anniversary with members of her family. The menu is a model of practicality, and one that would work just as impressively for eight or twelve, even if you don't have the same level of expert help in the kitchen.

The appetizer is one that is served at room temperature and can be arranged and garnished on plates before the guests arrive. None of the main-course dishes needs last-minute fussing in the kitchen: You might have the roast veal sliced and kept covered and warm in a slow oven, along with the asparagus and stuffed mushroom caps.

Chocolate Charlotte is one of those desserts you will want to be mysterious about. No one need know such an ornate and delicious confection was made quickly and effortlessly the day before.

Shrimp and Peapods Vinaigrette
Roast Rack of Veal with Ginger
Lemon Buttered Fresh Asparagus
Mushroom Caps Stuffed with Herbed Wild Rice
Dinner rolls
Frozen Chocolate Charlotte

SHRIMP AND PEAPODS VINAIGRETTE

Serves 12

1 teaspoon white vinegar
1 bouquet garni
  Water
3 pounds jumbo Gulf shrimp (see note)
1 teaspoon salt
½ teaspoon pepper
¾ pound peapods
1 cup Sweet-Pepper Vinaigrette (recipe
    follows)
1 cup sliced water chestnuts
1 small onion, finely chopped
  Parsley
8 radish roses
  Lemon wedges
  Watercress

Bring to a boil vinegar, bouquet garni, and enough water to cover shrimp. Drop in shrimp and return to boil. Turn off heat and let stand for 3 minutes. Drain; then refresh under cold water and pat dry with paper towel. Peel and devein shrimp, leaving on the tails and set aside.

Add salt and pepper to a fresh pot of boiling water. Blanch peapods. Drain and refresh with cold water. Put in a large bowl and add shrimp, vinaigrette, water chestnuts, and onion. Toss well, making sure shrimp and vegetables are well coated. Serve chilled, garnished with parsley, radish roses, lemon wedges, and watercress.

Note: *There are usually 10 to 14 Gulf shrimp per pound. If using a different variety, you can order by portion per person.*

SWEET-PEPPER VINAIGRETTE

Makes 1 cup

⅔ cup olive oil
⅓ cup red wine vinegar
¼ teaspoon minced red and green pepper
1 scallion, minced
1 teaspoon Dijon mustard
½ teaspoon sugar
  Salt and pepper

Put all ingredients except salt and pepper in a blender and mix well. Add salt and pepper to taste.

ROAST RACK OF VEAL WITH GINGER

Serves 12

1 eye of veal rack
1/2 cup fresh ground ginger
4 ounces butter
3 cups chicken or veal stock
1/4 teaspoon salt
1/4 ground pepper
1 bay leaf
1 small onion, chopped
1 tablespoon flour

Preheat oven to 475°.

Place eye of veal rack in roasting pan; sprinkle well with 1/4 cup of fresh ground ginger. Add 2 ounces butter, veal or chicken stock, salt, pepper, bay leaf and onion. Roast veal for 25 minutes. Remove meat from pan. Whisk flour into pan drippings. Add remaining ginger and cook 5 minutes. Strain into separate sauce pan. Add remaining butter, bring to boil until melted. To serve, slice veal thinly, spoon small amount sauce on hot plates; place veal on top of sauce, garnished with stuffed mushroom caps. Pass extra gravy separately.

LEMON BUTTERED FRESH ASPARAGUS

Serves 12

5 pounds fresh asparagus, peeled
1/2 teaspoon salt
1/2 teaspoon sugar
Boiling water
4 ounces butter
1 tablespoon lemon juice

Put asparagus in a stainless-steel pot with salt and sugar. Pour boiling water over asparagus. Return to a boil for 2 minutes. Drain. Add butter and lemon juice and mix thoroughly till butter is melted.

MUSHROOM CAPS STUFFED WITH HERBED WILD RICE

Serves 12

12 large mushrooms
1 1/2 cups wild rice
6 cups chicken broth
1 celery stalk, finely chopped
1/2 teaspoon salt
1/4 teaspoon pepper
1 small onion, chopped
4 ounces butter

Remove mushroom stems from caps and chop the stems coarsely, setting caps aside. Cover rice with half the broth. Add all ingredients except mushroom caps. Bring to boil and cook for three hours, adding remaining stock as the rice is cooking.

Preheat oven to 400°.

Fill mushroom caps with rice mixture. Put in a baking pan, cover, and bake for 7 minutes. *Do not overcook.* Mushrooms should be firm. Arrange around veal platter and serve.

FROZEN CHOCOLATE CHARLOTTE

Serves 12

8 ounces semisweet dark chocolate
8 ounces sweet dark chocolate
6 eggs, separated
1 cup Grand Marnier
½ cup extra strong coffee
  Grated rind of one orange
6 pints heavy whipping cream
3 boxes ladyfingers
1 cup sweet chocolate curls

Put chocolate in a large mixing bowl and melt over hot water. Remove from heat. In a separate bowl beat yolks with ½ cup Grand Marnier and coffee. Add to melted chocolate and mix well. Add orange rind.

In a separate bowl beat 3 pints of whipping cream until very thick. Beat egg whites until stiff and fold into chocolate mixture with whipped cream.

Line bottom and sides of a 10-inch spring-form pan with ladyfingers, and sprinkle evenly with remaining ½ cup Grand Marnier. Spoon in mousse, cover top with ladyfingers, and put in freezer for 8 hours or longer. Turn upside down on silver platter. Whip remaining cream and decorate mousse. Sprinkle with chocolate curls.

Note: *Except for decorations, recipe may be made several days in advance.*

A Brunch in Highlands, North Carolina

What better way to entertain than a house-party brunch—an informal, relaxed, and open-ended Sunday event. This one is lavish, a repast to satisfy a goodly number of guests, even if, as in this case, those partaking have whetted their appetites with a brisk morning walk in beautiful mountain country.

Hearty entrées range from rich Rainbow Trout with St. Simons Blue Crab Stuffing to down-home Country Stuffed Cabbage Leaves, and they include a marvelous specialty dish: Chicken, Shrimp, and Louisiana Pecan Rice Casserole. Accompaniments include a colorful vegetable medley and a variation on a Southern standby, Blanche's Spoonbread. The meal concludes with a refreshing, unusual dessert.

Rainbow Trout with St. Simons Blue Crab Stuffing
Country Stuffed Cabbage Leaves
Chicken, Shrimp, and Louisiana Pecan Rice Casserole
Stuffed Turkey Roll
Blanche's Spoonbread
Broiled Herbed Tomatoes
Onions, Red Peppers, and Garden Fresh String Beans in Dilled Vinaigrette
Apple Cider Sherbet with Raspberry Sauce

Rainbow Trout with St. Simons Blue Crab Stuffing

Serves 8

1/2 cup chopped onion
1/3 cup chopped celery
1/3 cup chopped green pepper
2 cloves garlic, crushed or grated
1/2 cup chopped pimiento
1/4 pound (1 stick) butter or margarine
1 pound blue crab claw meat, picked over
2 eggs, slightly beaten
1/2 teaspoon seafood seasoning
1 teaspoon salt
1/2 teaspoon pepper
1 teaspoon Worcestershire sauce (optional)
1 teaspoon horseradish (optional)
2 cups fresh bread crumbs
8 whole fresh rainbow trout, cleaned, with
    heads and tails left intact
Paprika

In a heavy skillet, sauté onion, celery, green pepper, garlic, and pimiento in butter. Remove from heat. Add crabmeat, eggs, seafood seasoning, salt, pepper, Worcestershire sauce, and horseradish. Stir in bread crumbs gradually until mixture holds together well. Adjust seasonings to taste.

Preheat broiler. Wipe the cavity of the trout with a damp paper towel. Dot with butter. Stuff cavities loosely with crabmeat mixture. Place the fish on their sides in a shallow baking pan greased with butter. Dot the skins with additional butter. Broil 3 to 5 inches from heat for 5 minutes. Sprinkle with paprika and additional bread crumbs, if you wish. Turn fish and broil about 5 minutes longer. Fish is cooked when meat flakes easily but is still moist.

Country Stuffed Cabbage Leaves

Serves 8

1 large head cabbage
1/2 cup rice
2 tablespoons vegetable oil
1 small onion, grated
1 pound ground beef
1/2 pound ground pork or veal
2 eggs
1 teaspoon salt
1/4 teaspoon pepper
2 cans (8 ounces each) tomato paste
1 cup tomato puree
1 cup water
1 large onion
1/4 cup vinegar (optional)
3 strips bacon, cooked and crumbled
    (optional)

Remove core from cabbage. Place cabbage right side up in 2 inches of boiling water. Steam 5 minutes. Remove cabbage, set aside to cool and carefully peel off outer leaves. Return cabbage to boiling water for 5 more minutes and peel off outer leaves again, repeating this procedure until you have removed all the leaves. Reserve 10 to 12 large, undamaged cabbage leaves to use as cover leaves.

Cook rice in boiling water for 10 minutes. Drain and immediately rinse with cold water. Drain again and set aside.

Heat the oil in a heavy skillet and cook the onion until it is wilted but not browned. Combine ground meat with eggs, rice, salt, and pepper. Add meat mixture to skillet and stir until the ingredients are thoroughly combined and the meat is browned. Refrigerate until cool enough to handle.

Place a meatball-size amount of meat mixture in one of the smaller cabbage leaves. Fold the edges of the leaf over the filling and tuck in the ends; set aside, seam side down.

Repeat until you have used all of the meat mixture.

Preheat oven to 325°. Line the bottom of a heavy baking dish or a Dutch oven with the remaining small cabbage leaves. Arrange stuffed cabbage leaves on top, seam side down. Stir together the tomato paste, tomato puree, and water and pour the mixture over the stuffed cabbage. Top with onion slices and add vinegar, if you wish. Bake, covered, 1 hour. (Can be refrigerated overnight at this point and finished before serving.)

Dip reserved large cabbage leaves in simmering water until barely wilted. Place 2 or 3 stuffed cabbage leaves in the center of each large leaf and fold sides and ends over to make a package. Place in serving dish, seam side down; repeat with remaining large leaves. Ladle sauce over stuffed cabbage. Top with crumbled bacon, if desired.

CHICKEN, SHRIMP, AND LOUISIANA PECAN RICE CASSEROLE

Serves 8

1 cup long-grained rice, preferably Louisiana Pecan Rice
3 whole chicken breasts, skinned, boned,
   and cut into bite-size pieces
4 tablespoons butter
   Salt and white pepper to taste
1½ pounds shrimp, shelled and deveined
   Juice of 1 lemon
3 cups Light Wine Sauce (recipe follows)
   or 2 cans cream of chicken or cream
   of mushroom soup thinned with 1
   can milk
½ cup day-old bread crumbs
1 cup cooked green beans or peas

Cook rice according to package
directions.

Season chicken with salt and white pepper and sauté lightly in butter.

Preheat oven to 325°. Drop shrimp into
boiling salted water with lemon juice. Cook
until pink, about 2 minutes. Drain and rinse
with cold water.

In buttered casserole combine rice,
chicken, and shrimp with Light Wine Sauce
or diluted soup. (Can be refrigerated overnight at this point and finished before serving.) Top with bread crumbs. Bake 15 to 20
minutes. Add hot green beans or peas and
spoon sauce over top to glaze vegetables.

LIGHT WINE SAUCE

Makes 3 cups

1 clove garlic, minced
3 tablespoons butter
3 tablespoons flour
2 cups chicken broth
1 cup dry white wine

Sauté garlic in butter until wilted but
not browned. Stir in flour and cook over low
heat for 2 minutes. Add broth slowly, stirring
constantly. Simmer 5 minutes. Add wine;
simmer 5 minutes longer.

STUFFED TURKEY ROLL

Serves 8

1 turkey breast, boned, skin left on
⅜ pound (1½ sticks) butter, softened
1 pound thinly sliced Virginia ham or
   prosciutto
2 cups chopped parsley
2 cups chopped sweet red pepper

Lightly pound the meaty side of the
breast into an approximation of a rectangle.
Spread with ¼ pound (1 stick) of the butter.
Remove rind, if any, from ham slices and lay
the slices over one half of the meaty side of
the turkey. Spread a layer of parsley and then
a layer of chopped peppers on top of the
ham.

Preheat oven to 350°. Roll up the turkey, or fold it over and secure the skin at the seams with toothpicks. Rub with remaining butter. Bake 45 minutes, basting once with pan juices. Refrigerate. Remove toothpicks and slice thinly before serving. (May be prepared ahead of time and refrigerated up to 3 days.)

BLANCHE'S SPOONBREAD

Serves 8

1 cup self-rising cornmeal
3 cups milk
2 tablespoons butter
3 eggs
 Salt to taste
2 tablespoons sugar, or more, to taste

Preheat oven to 400°.

In a heavy saucepan, mix the cornmeal with 2 cups milk, reserving the remaining cup milk. Place over medium heat and cook, stirring, until mixture begins to thicken; add butter and stir until mixture is smooth.

Beat together the eggs, salt, sugar, and remaining milk. Add to cornmeal mixture. Pour into buttered 1½-quart casserole or baking pan. Bake 30 to 35 minutes or until spoonbread feels firm in the center and top is richly browned.

Broiled Herbed Tomatoes

Serves 8

8 large tomatoes, cored and halved but
    not peeled
$1/4$ cup ($1/2$ stick) butter
    Salt and pepper to taste
$1/2$ cup bread crumbs
$1/2$ cup chopped parsley
$1/2$ cup chopped chives

Preheat broiler. Arrange tomato halves on a cookie sheet or in a baking pan, cut side up. Place about $1/2$ teaspoon butter on each tomato half. Sprinkle with salt and pepper, bread crumbs, parsley, and chives. Broil 5 to 7 minutes, until lightly browned and bubbling.

Onions, Red Peppers, and Garden Fresh String Beans in Dilled Vinaigrette

Serves 8

2 pounds fresh string beans
    Salt to taste
1 large onion

3 sweet red peppers
$1/3$ cup salad oil
$1/4$ cup wine vinegar
$1/2$ teaspoon salt
$1/4$ teaspoon pepper
3 tablespoons chopped fresh dill

Plunge string beans into rapidly boiling water with salt to taste and cook 7 minutes. Drain, and refresh in cold water.

Cut onion and red peppers into thin slices; toss with green beans.

Thoroughly combine oil, vinegar, salt, pepper, and dill. Pour over vegetables.

Apple Cider Sherbet with Raspberry Sauce

Serves 8

4 teaspoons grated lemon rind
4 cups sugar
8 cups unfiltered apple cider
$1/2$ teaspoon salt
$1/2$ cup lemon juice
$1/4$ cup applejack brandy
    Raspberry Sauce (recipe follows)

In a large saucepan, combine lemon rind, sugar, cider, and salt. Bring to a boil, stirring constantly. Reduce heat and simmer 5 minutes without stirring. Chill; add lemon juice and applejack.

To freeze mixture, pour it into a shallow pan and place in freezer until crystals begin to form. Remove, stir mixture thoroughly, put back in freezer. Repeat this process two more times before allowing sherbet to freeze and set completely.

Serve with Raspberry Sauce (recipe follows).

RASPBERRY SAUCE

Makes 2 cups

2 cups fresh or frozen raspberries
$^1/_3$ cup sugar or more, to taste
$^1/_4$ teaspoon vanilla
1 tablespoon cornstarch

Combine all ingredients and bring to a boil, stirring constantly. Reduce heat and simmer about 7 minutes.

Black-and-White Theme Dinner

A menu with a specific theme stirs the creative juices of the adventurous cook. If it's a menu to tie in with a color scheme, then the challenge is even greater. For a black-and-white black-tie party, setting the stage is easy: shiny black oilcloth coverings for the table; white napkins and plates; black candles set in white ceramic holders; and black containers holding arrangements of white gerbera daisies, freesia, roses, and sprays of white dendrobium orchids.

Such an evening would, of course, begin with caviar and end with chocolate. But what comes in between? New York caterer Mark Fahrer suggests a Turban of Sole, Nutted Rice, and a garnish of Mushroom Caps Stuffed with Black-eyed Peas.

Irish coffee or iced cappuccino following dessert would be an appropriate finale for such an unusual repast.

Endive and Black Caviar
Turban of Sole
Nutted Rice
Mushroom Caps Stuffed with Black-eyed Peas
Checkerboard Torte Filled with White Chocolate Mousse

ENDIVE AND BLACK CAVIAR

Serves 6

3 endives
4 white radishes, sliced
2 dozen black olives
3 ounces imported black caviar
  Melba toast, cut in triangles
1 bunch watercress

Fan out 4 endive leaves for each serving. Put a half teaspoon of caviar on top of each leaf. Garnish the plate with radishes, olives, melba toast, and watercress.

TURBAN OF SOLE

Serves 6

1½ pounds raw shrimp, peeled and
    deveined
2 egg whites
  Salt and pepper
½ cup heavy cream
½ teaspoon chopped dill
2 tablespoons butter
8 large, thin fillets of sole
  Sprigs of fresh dill

Reserve 6 large shrimp. Put remaining shrimp into the container of a food processor and process until smooth. Add egg whites and process for about 10 seconds. Add salt, pepper, and heavy cream. Process just until smooth. Transfer puree to a mixing bowl. Stir in dill. Refrigerate for 30 minutes.

Preheat oven to 325°. Butter a ring mold heavily. Line mold with sole fillets, overlapping them slightly and allowing ends to hang over edges of mold. Fill lined mold with shrimp mixture. Fold ends of fillets over the top of the shrimp mousse. Cover with foil.

Set the mold in a pan of hot water that comes two thirds of the way up the sides of the mold. Bake about 45 minutes. Remove from oven and let rest for 10 minutes.

While mold is resting, butterfly remaining shrimp and steam over boiling water for 5 minutes. Unmold turban onto serving platter. Arrange steamed shrimp around edges. Garnish with fresh dill.

NUTTED RICE

2 tablespoons butter
1 medium onion, minced
2 cups rice
½ cup toasted, slivered almonds
4 cups chicken stock
  Salt and pepper to taste

In a saucepan melt butter and cook onion until wilted. Stir in rice and almonds. Add stock, and salt and pepper to taste. Bring to a boil. Cover and simmer until liquid is absorbed, about 15 minutes.

MUSHROOM CAPS STUFFED WITH BLACK-EYED PEAS

Serves 8

8 large mushrooms, blanched, with stems
    removed
1 cup black-eyed peas, soaked overnight in
    water
2 cups chicken stock
4 ounces ham, finely chopped
3 tablespoons butter, melted

Add ham to black-eyed peas and simmer in stock until tender. Mix in melted butter and fill mushroom caps with the mixture. Run under broiler to heat.

CHECKERBOARD TORTE FILLED WITH WHITE CHOCOLATE MOUSSE

Serves 8

CAKE

1¹/₂ ounces baking chocolate
2¹/₂ cups sifted cake flour
  3 teaspoons baking powder
³/₄ teaspoon salt
³/₄ cup butter, softened
1¹/₂ cups sugar
1¹/₂ teaspoons vanilla
  3 eggs separated
³/₄ cup milk

WHITE CHOCOLATE MOUSSE

8 ounces white chocolate
6 egg yolks
4 ounces butter
¹/₂ cup crème de cacao
1 quart heavy whipping cream
¹/₄ cup sugar
    Chocolate Butter Icing (recipe follows)

Grease bottoms of three 8-inch cake pans. Line with 8-inch rounds of wax paper and grease the paper.

Preheat oven to 350°.

Melt chocolate in a saucepan and cool slightly. Sift together flour, baking powder, and salt. Set aside. Cream butter until fluffy. Add sugar gradually. Beat well after each addition so that sugar crystals dissolve. Add vanilla and egg yolks and beat until well blended. Add dry ingredients and milk alternately in parts. Beat well after each addition. Beat egg whites until stiff and fold into batter. Divide batter into thirds and add melted chocolate to one portion. Bake in prepared pans for 25 minutes.

To make mousse, melt chocolate and butter in a double boiler. Stir in egg yolks and crème de cacao. Let cool. Whip heavy cream with sugar and fold into cooled chocolate. Spread between cake layers and frost with Chocolate Butter Icing.

CHOCOLATE BUTTER ICING

3 ounces baking chocolate
6 tablespoons milk
3 cups confectioners' sugar
6 tablespoons butter, softened
  Pinch of salt
1 tablespoon vanilla

Melt chocolate in a double boiler. Heat milk to boiling, remove from heat, and add confectioners' sugar all at once. Beat until smooth. Add melted chocolate and cool to lukewarm. Beat butter until creamy. Beat in salt, vanilla, and cooled chocolate. Spread on cake at once.

A Benefit Luncheon in Central Park's Conservatory Garden

If you have ever served on a benefit committee, you are probably aware of how difficult it can be to keep coming up with fresh, new ideas for fund-raising events. What better way—or simpler—than to take the festivities outdoors, where nature has done the party decorating for you. A luncheon in late spring or early fall—whether in an elegant conservatory garden, on the lawn of a country club, or in the back garden of a church hall—is sure to have a backdrop that includes a profusion of colors richer and more splendid than any committee could devise.

This menu is a simple one composed of elegant dishes, from the chilled Cream of Avocado Soup to the Chilled Strawberry Soufflé. Everything on the bill of fare, including the salad, vegetable accompaniment, and flavored butter to complement a crisp bread, can be made ahead of time for serving outdoors with an absolute minimum of effort. This means, of course, that even the committee members will enjoy themselves right along with the guests.

Note that for manageability, recipes are given in servings of ten, so you can multiply as required or prepare dishes in batches.

Cream of Avocado Soup
Curried Chicken and Shrimp Salad
Asparagus Tips Vinaigrette
Baguettes   Watercress Butter
Chilled Strawberry Soufflé

106

CREAM OF AVOCADO SOUP

Serves 10

1 cup minced onion
4 tablespoons butter
4 tablespoons flour
6 cups chicken broth
2 tablespoons fresh lemon juice
2 tablespoons drained prepared horseradish
2 tablespoons tarragon vinegar
2 cloves garlic, crushed
1/4 teaspoon curry powder
1/2 teaspoon dried tarragon
   Salt
   Freshly ground white pepper
2 ripe avocados
2 cups milk
2 cups light cream

In a large saucepan, sauté the onion in butter until transparent. Add the flour and stir until smooth. Stir in 3 cups broth and cook, stirring constantly, until it boils and thickens. Add the lemon juice, horseradish, vinegar, garlic, curry powder, tarragon, and salt and pepper to taste. Simmer, covered, for 10 minutes. Puree the mixture in a food mill, blender, or food processor and return it to the pan. Peel the avocados with a stainless-steel knife to prevent darkening and puree with the with the remaining cups broth. Add the puree to the pan and stir in the milk and cream. Cook, stirring, until the soup is heated through. Serve hot or cold in glass bowls.

CURRIED CHICKEN AND SHRIMP SALAD

Serves 10

1 cup mayonnaise
1 1/2 cups sour cream
2 tablespoons Dijon mustard
1 teaspoon curry powder
2 cloves garlic, finely chopped
3 cups cold, cooked rice
   Dry white wine or water
2 cups cold cooked chicken, in chunks
1 pound cold cooked shrimp, shelled and
   deveined
2 red peppers cut into julienne strips
2 green peppers cut into julienne strips
1 cup sliced leek, white part only
3 endives

In a bowl, combine the mayonnaise, sour cream, mustard, curry powder, and garlic and blend thoroughly. Add the rice, toss, and add a little white wine or water to thin the mixture, if necessary. Add the chicken, shrimp, peppers, and leek. Toss gently and adjust the seasonings. Transfer the salad to a glass platter lined with endive leaves and serve chilled or at room temperature.

ASPARAGUS TIPS VINAIGRETTE

Serves 10

4 pounds asparagus
1/3 cup white wine vinegar
1 cup vegetable oil
1/2 cup sliced scallions (with some green tops)
2 tablespoon chopped parsley
1 tablespoon sugar
   Salt and pepper to taste
   Leaf lettuce (Boston or romaine)

   Wash the asparagus and break off the tough ends. With a vegetable parer, remove the scales and skin from the lower portion of each stalk. Place asparagus in a steamer over boiling water, cover, and steam for 15 minutes, or until just tender. Plunge the asparagus into a large bowl of ice and water to chill it quickly and stop the cooking. Drain the asparagus, wrap in paper towel, and refrigerate until serving time. Combine the vinegar, oil, scallions, parsley, sugar, salt, and pepper in a small bowl. Refrigerate, covered, for at least 1 hour. To serve, arrange the asparagus on a bed of lettuce and spoon the vinaigrette dressing over it.

WATERCRESS BUTTER

Makes 2 1/2 cups

1 1/4 pounds (5 sticks) unsalted butter, softened
1 bunch watercress, leaves only, minced
2 tablespoons lemon juice
1 teaspoon salt
   Freshly ground black pepper to taste

   Cream the butter by mashing it against the sides of the bowl with a wooden spoon until it is light and fluffy. Add the other ingredients, blending well. Serve with sliced breads.
   Note: *Watercress butter will keep in the refrigerator, in a tightly covered container, for 2 weeks. It can be shaped into a cylinder by rolling in a sheet of waxed paper. Refrigerate to harden slightly or freeze until needed.*

CHILLED STRAWBERRY SOUFFLÉ

Serves 10

2 1/2 pints strawberries, washed and hulled
2 tablespoons unflavored gelatin
3/4 cup sugar
1/2 cup water
1 1/2 tablespoons lemon juice
2 tablespoons kirsch
4 egg whites
1 1/2 cups heavy cream, stiffly beaten

Make an oiled aluminum-foil collar for a 4-cup soufflé dish. Reserve 8 of the most attractive berries to use as a garnish. Puree the remaining berries in a food processor. If you wish, put the puree through a sieve to remove the seeds. In a saucepan mix the gelatin and 1/2 cup of the sugar with the water and place over low heat to dissolve. Add the gelatin, juice, and the kirsch to the berries. Refrigerate the mixture until it thickens slightly (about 30 minutes). Beat the egg whites until foamy. Gradually add the remaining 1/4 cup sugar and beat until stiff. Fold the beaten egg whites into the strawberries. Fold in the whipped cream. Pour into the soufflé dish and refrigerate until firm, about 4 hours. Garnish with the reserved strawberries.

A Luncheon in the Historic District
of Charleston

From the Layered Seafood Pâté to the Lemon Bavarian Cream with Strawberry Sauce, this delicious repast was the perfect way for a Southern couple to honor their out-of-town guests. Although many of these dishes can be thought of as indigenous to the South, they are as appropriate for a lunch in Manhattan as they were for this Charleston gathering. You may want to prepare several of these dishes in advance: The flounder fillets can be cooked one day beforehand, and the dough for the rolls can be refrigerated for five days before baking. The delicious cured ham is a special treat, and though it requires two to three days' preparation time, it can be served at room temperature, which means the oven will be available for baking other dishes directly before the meal.

Layered Seafood Pâté
She-Crab Soup
Fillets of Flounder Primavera
Southern-style Country-Cured Ham
Freshly Baked Rolls
Squash Medley   Carrots with Almonds and Pineapple
Lemon Bavarian Cream with Strawberry Sauce

LAYERED SEAFOOD PÂTÉ

Serves 8

FISH LAYER

1/2 pound flounder or firm white fish
1/4 cup dry vermouth
1 teaspoon Tabasco
1 teaspoon beau monde
2 tablespoons finely chopped onion
1 tablespoon lemon juice
8 ounces cream cheese, softened
 Salt and pepper to taste
1 tablespoon gelatin

Poach fish in vermouth and enough water to cover with Tabasco, beau monde, onion, and lemon juice. Remove fish and reduce liquid to half a cup. Let cool. Soften gelatin in cooled stock; then heat to dissolve. Process fish and cream cheese in bowl of a food processor until well mixed. Gradually add gelatin mixture.

SPINACH LAYER

10 ounces frozen spinach
3 scallions, sliced
4 tablespoons butter
1 tablespoon gelatin
8 ounces cream cheese, softened
1/2 teaspoon ground nutmeg
1 teaspoon Lawry's seasoned salt
1/2 teaspoon Tabasco
 Salt and pepper to taste

Thaw spinach and drain. Sauté spinach and scallions in butter. Soften gelatin in 1/4 cup water and heat to dissolve. Place cream cheese and seasonings in a food processor and process until smooth. Add salt and pepper to taste.

SHRIMP LAYER

1/2 pound shrimp, peeled and deveined
4 tablespoons butter
1 teaspoon dehydrated onion flakes
1 teaspoon lemon juice
1/2 teaspoon Worcestershire sauce
1/4 teaspoon Tabasco
1 teaspoon celery salt
1 tablespoon gelatin
8 ounces cream cheese, softened
 Salt and pepper to taste

Sauté shrimp in butter until just barely pink. Stir in onion flakes and seasonings. Soften gelatin in 1/4 cup water and heat to dissolve. Put in bowl of food processor with shrimp and cream cheese and process until smooth. Add salt and pepper to taste.

To assemble the pâté, spray a 2-quart fish mold with vegetable-oil spray. Carefully spoon in fish layer. Chill until set. Follow with spinach layer and shrimp layer, chilling after each addition. To unmold, place mold in warm water up to the edges for 30 seconds. Turn out on a large platter. Place reserved whole shrimp around edge of platter. Decorate top with sprigs of parsley and strips of pimiento.

SHE-CRAB SOUP

Serves 8

4 tablespoons butter
$^1/_4$ cup flour
6 cups milk
1 teaspoon Worcestershire sauce
$^3/_4$ teaspoon beau monde or celery salt
$^1/_4$ teaspoon white pepper
1 teaspoon Tabasco
1 tablespoon dehydrated onion flakes
1 pound white crabmeat, shredded
$^1/_2$ cup, or more, dry sherry
  Mace
  Lemon slices
  Parsley
  Whole crayfish (optional)

Melt butter in heavy saucepan, whisk in flour, and cook over medium heat for 2 minutes, to make a roux. Add milk gradually, whisking constantly. Add seasonings and cook over medium heat until mixture comes to a boil, stirring constantly. Stir in crabmeat and sherry. Simmer 5 minutes. Sprinkle mace on top. Decorate with twisted lemon slice, sprig parsley, and whole crayfish if desired.

Note: *If in season, crab roe is an ideal garnish.*

FILLETS OF FLOUNDER PRIMAVERA

Serves 8

30-40 small spears asparagus (fresh or
    frozen)
8 6-ounce flounder fillets, or any firm
    white fish
  Celery salt
  White pepper
$^1/_4$ pound (1 stick) butter, melted
  Paprika
  Parsley
  Grapes
  Orange slices
  Shrimp Sauce (recipe follows)
  Wild Rice (see "Cook's Miscellany"
    section)

Preheat oven to 325°.

Cook asparagus until just tender. Season fillets with celery salt and pepper and brush with melted butter. Roll each fillet around 3 to 5 asparagus spears and place seam side down in an oiled roasting pan. Cover with foil and bake 15 to 20 minutes or until fish is opaque. Brush fillets with butter and sprinkle with paprika. Serve with Shrimp Sauce.

SHRIMP SAUCE

6 tablespoons butter
1 pound shrimp, peeled and deveined
6 tablespoons flour

CARROTS WITH ALMONDS AND PINEAPPLE

Serves 8

3 pounds carrots, pared and sliced ¹/₂
  inch thick
4 tablespoons butter
¹/₂ teaspoon ginger
¹/₂ teaspoon Tabasco
1 cup whole almonds
1 16-ounce can pineapple tidbits

Steam carrots until tender but still crisp. Melt butter in a sauté pan. Stir in ginger and Tabasco. Toss almonds and pineapple in butter. Add carrots and coat with butter. Serve immediately.

¹/₂ cup dry vermouth
2 cups milk
1 teaspoon beau monde or celery salt
1 teaspoon Tabasco

Melt butter and sauté shrimp until pink. Remove from pan with slotted spoon. Whisk in flour and cook, stirring, to make a roux. Gradually stir in vermouth and milk and seasonings. Cook over medium heat, stirring constantly, until mixture comes to a boil again. Reserve several shrimp for garnish; chop the rest and add to sauce.

To arrange, place flounder rolls on a bed of rice and mushrooms. Garnish serving platter with shrimp, orange slices, parsley sprigs, and concord or green grapes. (See photo.)

Note: *Fillets may be cooked one day in advance. Paint with melted butter to prevent drying out.*

Easy Refrigerator Roll Dough

Makes 1 dozen rolls

1 package active dry yeast
1 1/2 cups warm water (105-115°)
1 cup unseasoned mashed potatoes, warm
3/4 cup sugar
3/4 cup butter
2 eggs
1 1/2 teaspoons salt
6-7 1/2 cups all-purpose flour

Dissolve yeast in a large bowl of warm water. Stir in potatoes, sugar, butter, eggs, salt, and three cups of flour. Beat until smooth. Mix in enough additional flour to make dough easy to handle—not sticky. Turn dough onto lightly floured surface and knead until smooth and elastic, about 5 to 10 minutes. Put dough in a greased bowl and paint with oil. Cover bowl tightly with plastic wrap. Refrigerate at least 8 hours or up to 5 days.

Punch down dough and divide into four pieces. Roll each piece of dough into a 12 × 9-inch rectangle on a well-floured surface. Cut into 3-inch circles. Brush with melted butter. Make crease across center. Fold over so that top half of roll slightly overlaps bottom. Press edges together and place close together in a greased 9 × 9-inch pan. Brush with melted butter. Let rise 1 hour. Preheat oven to 400°. Bake 15 to 20 minutes or until golden brown.

Southern-style Country-Cured Ham

Serves 20 or more

1 12- to 16-pound ham
1 pound dark-brown sugar
1/2 gallon apple cider
Water
1 cup dry sherry
2 cups light-brown sugar
1 cup cornmeal
1 teaspoon dry mustard
1 teaspoon coarsely ground pepper
1 fresh pineapple, halved
1 bunch scallions, feathered
Spiced apple rings
Parsley

Scrub ham and soak in cool water for 48 hours, changing water 3-4 times. Place ham in a large kettle with dark-brown sugar, apple cider, and enough water to cover ham. Bring to a boil and reduce heat. Simmer 20 minutes per pound. Allow ham to cool in liquid. When cool, remove skin and all but a very thin layer of fat.

Mix together sherry and 1 cup light-brown sugar. Pierce ham all over with a fork and rub sherry mixture into surface. Mix together cornmeal, remaining light-brown sugar, mustard, and pepper and coat ham surface thoroughly. Place ham in preheated 350° oven for about 30 minutes or until coating begins to brown. May be served warm or at room temperature. Place ham on a bed of parsley on a large platter. Surround with spiced apple rings, feathered scallions, and pineapple halves. (See photo.)

SQUASH MEDLEY

Serves 8

2 tablespoons butter
1¹/2 pounds zucchini, thinly sliced
1¹/2 pounds yellow squash, thinly sliced
1 small onion, finely chopped
Crazy Jane's Mixed Up Salt

Melt butter in a skillet and sauté squash and onions until crisply tender. Season to taste.

LEMON BAVARIAN CREAM WITH STRAWBERRY SAUCE

Serves 8

1 tablespoon unflavored gelatin
¹/4 cup cold water

8 ounces cream cheese
¹/4 cup freshly squeezed lemon juice
1 tablespoon finely grated lemon rind
¹/2 cup sugar
³/4 cup milk
1 cup heavy cream
Strawberry Sauce (recipe follows)

Soften the gelatin in cold water and heat to dissolve. Combine cream cheese with lemon juice, rind, and sugar. Mix until well blended. Gradually add milk and dissolved gelatin. Chill until slightly thickened. Pour into a 1¹/2-quart bowl or mold and chill until firm. Or, spoon into stemmed dessert glasses, layering with sauce, if desired. Decorate with whipped cream.

STRAWBERRY SAUCE

1 quart whole strawberries
2 tablespoons sugar
2 tablespoons cornstarch
¹/2 cup water
³/4 cup orange marmalade
2 tablespoons triple sec or apricot brandy

Mash 1 cup strawberries; cut rest into halves. Combine sugar and cornstarch in a saucepan and gradually add water. Stir in mashed strawberries, marmalade, and liqueur. Cook, stirring constantly, over moderate heat until mixture comes to a boil and becomes clear and thick. Cool slightly and stir in remaining strawberries. Serve hot or cold.

A Kentucky Derby Party

You don't have to live in the South to celebrate on the day of the Derby. The oldest annual sporting event in the United States is as fine an excuse for a party in Maine or Arizona as in Kentucky. The recipes presented here were chosen because they capture the spirit of the "most exciting two minutes in American sports." Mint Juleps, of course, are crucial. Traditionally they are served in chilled silver julep cups, which will frost on the outside when filled with the julep mixture. If you can't put your hands on a set of silver mugs, use 10-ounce glasses. The bourbon, however, must be 100 proof. No substitute will produce the proper amount of glistening frost on the glasses.

The foods presented here are all but indigenous to the South, from assorted finger sandwiches right down to the Rum Balls and Bourbon Pound Cake. All of the favorites are here in abundance: cream cheese, shrimp, ham, pecans, mint, biscuits, bourbon, and rum. What could be more appropriate fare for Derby Day?

Mint Juleps   Minted Iced Tea
Open-faced Sandwiches
Marinated Shrimp
Ham Mousse   Pumpernickel, Rye, and White Bread Triangles
Cheese Pecan Biscuits
Rum Balls   Bourbon Pound Cake

MINT JULEPS

Makes 12 juleps

7 pounds crushed ice
1¹/₂ cups water
4 cups sugar
1 large bunch fresh mint
3 cups 100-proof bourbon

Place mint-julep mugs in freezer for 2 to 3 hours; remove, fill with ice, and return to freezer for at least 6 hours or overnight.

Mix water and sugar in a saucepan; bring to a boil and simmer until syrupy. Reserve 12 of the most attractive mint sprigs and place remaining sprigs in sugar syrup. Set mixture aside until completely cool. Put syrup through a medium sieve and discard mint.

A few minutes before serving time, take julep mugs out of freezer, leaving ice in them. Pour ¹/₄ cup syrup and then ¹/₄ cup bourbon into each glass, and stir slightly. Garnish with reserved mint sprigs. Serve at once.

MINTED ICED TEA

Makes 20 servings

4 quarts cold water
6 tablespoons tea
1 quart orange juice
8 tablespoons lemon juice (about 4
    lemons)
1¹/₂ cups sugar

4 sticks cinnamon
15 sprigs mint
Additional mint sprigs for garnish

In a large enameled or stainless-steel saucepan, bring 2 of the 4 cups of cold water and the tea to a boil, and let it steep. Pour into a large pitcher and reserve. Add remaining 2 quarts water, orange juice, lemon juice, and sugar to the saucepan. Tie mint sprigs and cinnamon sticks in cheesecloth and add to the juice mixture. Bring to a boil and simmer gently for 1 hour. Remove cheesecloth and add prepared tea to the mixture.

OPEN-FACE SANDWICHES

Makes approximately 150–200 canapés

1 loaf pumpernickel, thinly sliced, crusts
    removed
1 loaf firm white bread, thinly sliced,
    crusts removed
1 loaf unseeded rye bread, thinly sliced,
    crusts removed
Sweet or lightly salted butter
2¹/₂ cups Liver Pâté (recipe follows)
Fresh dill, cut into small sprigs
Ripe olives, sliced
2¹/₂ cups Benedictine Sandwich Spread
    (recipe follows)
Pimiento strips
Watercress, cut into small sprigs

2¹/₂ cups Mushroom Spread (recipe follows)
Grated lemon rind
2¹/₂ cups Marinated Shrimp (recipe follows)

Spread butter thinly on one side of each slice of bread. Using cookie cutters or a sharp knife, cut bread into various shapes in appropriate sizes for finger sandwiches. Spread a fourth of the bread cutouts with Liver Pâté; garnish with dill sprigs, olive slices, and capers. Spread another fourth of cutouts with Benedictine Sandwich Spread; garnish with pimiento and watercress. Spread half of the remaining cutouts with Mushroom Spread; garnish with grated lemon rind. Place 1 or 2 Marinated Shrimp on each of the remaining cutouts; garnish with dill sprigs, olive slices, and capers.

LIVER PÂTÉ

4 4¹/₂-ounce cans prepared liver pâté
2 tablespoons grated onion
4 hard-cooked eggs, minced
Salt and pepper to taste

Combine pâté, grated onion, eggs, salt, and pepper. Refrigerate.

BENEDICTINE SANDWICH SPREAD

2 medium cucumbers, peeled and seeded
12 ounces cream cheese, softened to room
temperature
1 small onion, grated
Salt to taste
Mayonnaise

Grate cucumbers. Combine with cream cheese. Blend in onion and salt. Stir in enough mayonnaise to make spread the consistency you desire.

MUSHROOM SPREAD

¹/₂ pound mushrooms
¹/₄ cup chicken broth
1 3-ounce chicken pâté
1 tablespoon mayonnaise
¹/₂ tablespoon lemon juice
1 teaspoon chopped chives
¹/₄ teaspoon salt
1 teaspoon grated onion
1 drop hot pepper sauce (or to taste)

Cook mushrooms in broth 5 minutes; drain and mince. Stir in chicken pâté, mayonnaise, lemon juice, chives, salt, onion, and hot pepper sauce. Refrigerate.

MARINATED SHRIMP

2 cups small shrimp, shelled, deveined,
    and cooked
1/2 cup white wine vinegar
1/4 cup vegetable oil
1 teaspoon salt
1 small clove garlic, halved lengthwise
3 tablespoons chopped chives

Combine all ingredients; stir to coat shrimp well. Cover and refrigerate overnight.

HAM MOUSSE

Serves 12

4 envelopes unflavored gelatin
1/3 cup water
2 2/3 cups chicken broth
3 eggs, separated
7 cups cooked country-cured ham,
    ground
2 cups heavy cream
    Pumpernickel bread

Sprinkle gelatin into water to soften. Bring chicken broth to a boil. Remove from heat. Beat egg yolks lightly; stir in about 1/8 cup hot broth and pour egg-yolk mixture into remaining broth. Add gelatin and stir until it dissolves. Fold in ham. Reserve.

In separate bowls, beat egg whites and

cream until stiff. Fold egg whites and then cream into ham mixture. Rinse a 2-quart mold, or two 1-quart molds with cold water. While molds are still wet, spoon in mousse and refrigerate several hours or overnight, until firm. Serve with pumpernickel (or other bread) triangles.

CHEESE PECAN BISCUITS

Makes 12 to 16 biscuits

2 cups all-purpose flour
1 tablespoon baking powder
3/4 teaspoon salt
1/4 cup vegetable shortening
3/4 cup milk
4 tablespoons butter, melted
2/3 cup grated Cheddar cheese
1/2 cup chopped pecans

Preheat oven to 450°.

Sift flour, baking powder, and salt together. Cut in shortening. Pour in about 2/3 cup of the milk and all the butter. Stir dough with a fork. Dough should pull away from sides of bowl; add remaining milk if mixture is crumbly. Mix in cheese and nuts. Place dough on floured surface and knead for about 30 seconds. Roll out to 1/2-inch thickness. Cut dough with small, floured biscuit cutter. Place biscuits on ungreased cookie sheet. Bake until golden, 10 to 12 minutes.

Dough may be prepared ahead and wrapped and frozen.

RUM BALLS

Makes about 50

3 cups finely crushed vanilla wafers
1 cup finely chopped pecans
1/2 cup rum or bourbon
1 cup confectioners' sugar
1/2 cup cocoa
3 tablespoons light corn syrup
1 cup shredded coconut

Combine crushed wafers and chopped nuts. In a separate bowl, thoroughly mix rum or bourbon, sugar, cocoa, and corn syrup. Stir rum mixture into wafers and pecans. Shape into 1 1/2-inch balls and roll in shredded coconut. Refrigerate.

BOURBON POUND CAKE

Serves about 20

3/4 pound (3 sticks) butter
2 cups sugar
2 1/4 cups firmly packed light-brown sugar
8 eggs
5 cups sifted all-purpose flour
1/4 teaspoon salt
1 teaspoon mace
1 1/2 cups bourbon
3 1/2 cups (1 pound) coarsely chopped pecans

Preheat oven to 300°. Cream butter until soft. Thoroughly combine white and light-brown sugars. Gradually work half the sugar into the butter, keeping mixture as smooth as possible. In a separate bowl, beat the eggs until light and fluffy. Slowly beat in remaining sugar until mixture is smooth and creamy. Stir egg-sugar mixture into creamed butter and sugar; mix thoroughly.

Sift flour, salt, and mace together. Add flour mixture and bourbon to batter, alternating them (stirring after each addition), and beginning and ending with flour. Stir in pecans.

Pour into a well-greased 10-inch tube pan (batter should almost fill pan). Bake 1 1/2 to 1 3/4 hours, until sides of cake shrink slightly away from pan. Cool in pan about 15 minutes; turn out on cake rack and cool completely.

An Après-Tennis Party

What better way to thank your partner and console (or congratulate) your opponents than an après-tennis buffet? Invite other members of the club, too, if you like; the more the merrier when the fare for your repast can be prepared ahead and made ready to serve in a short time. Offer your guests a refreshing drink to enjoy while you attend to last-minute details in the kitchen. Take advantage of the season and serve outdoors, providing a relaxed atmosphere in which your guests can unwind and recover from the stresses of competition and exercise.

Serve a summer soup of carrots or spring peas prepared the night before and placed in the refrigerator to chill, accompanied by assorted appetizers, such as Miniature Quiches and Shrimp Salad Tarts, which can be popped in the oven for a short time when you return from the courts. Follow the first course with a selection of salads, both hearty and light. Provide a cooling summer punch, with or without alcohol, and round out your repast with beautiful summer fruits and luscious cheeses.

Sparkling Fruit Punch
Minted Pea Soup
Miniature Quiches
Zucchini and Rice Salad
Marinated Broccoli
Tomatoes Stuffed with Smoked Salmon
Fruit and Cheese with Wine

SPARKLING FRUIT PUNCH

Makes 5 quarts

2 quarts cranberry juice cocktail
1/2 pint strawberries, washed, hulled, and
   halved
1 orange, sectioned
1 1/2 quarts ginger ale
1 1/2 quarts sparkling water

Place in a punch bowl enough ice to chill the punch without diluting it. Pour in cranberry juice cocktail. Add strawberry halves and orange slices. Pour ginger ale and sparkling water gently into the fruit juice just before serving.

MINTED PEA SOUP

4 servings

4 cups green peas, fresh or frozen
1 medium onion, thinly sliced
2 cups water
4 tablespoons all-purpose flour
6 cups Chicken Stock or canned chicken
   broth
1 cup heavy cream
   Salt and freshly ground black pepper
   Finely chopped fresh mint

Cook the peas and onion in the water until they are tender. In a large saucepan whisk together the flour and 1 cup of the stock or broth until smooth. Add the remaining stock and cook, stirring until it is thickened. Puree the peas and onions with the water in which they were cooked in a food mill, blender, or food processor and add the puree to the stock. Bring to a boil, add the cream, and season with salt and pepper to taste. Chill the soup and serve it with mint. If soup is too thick, stir in more cream.

MINIATURE QUICHES
Makes 24 quiches

Plain Tart Crust (see "Cook's
    Miscellany" section)
1 egg white, mixed with 1 tablespoon
    water
2 eggs, lightly beaten
1 cup light cream
    Dash of salt
1 cup grated Swiss-type cheese
1/4 pound bacon, cooked, drained, and
    crumbled
    Dash of nutmeg

Roll half of the prepared tart crust to 1/8-inch thickness. Using a cookie cutter, cut the dough into 3 1/2-inch rounds. Carefully fit each round into a muffin-pan cup. Repeat the procedure with the remaining dough. Brush each pastry shell with the egg-white mixture and refrigerate until ready to fill.

Preheat oven to 400°. In a small bowl, combine the eggs, cream, salt, and nutmeg. To bake, sprinkle some grated cheese into each tart shell; spoon the egg and cream mixture over the cheese and bake for 20 minutes, or until the crust is golden and the filling is slightly puffed. Cool the quiches in the pans for 10 minutes, then remove them to a serving tray and sprinkle them with the bacon.

ZUCCHINI AND RICE SALAD
Serves 8

5 tablespoons olive oil
4 medium zucchini, coarsely chopped
1 medium onion, finely chopped
2 cloves garlic, finely chopped
1 1/2 cups cold cooked rice
1 cup chopped parsley
6-8 fresh basil leaves, finely chopped, or 1/2
    teaspoon dried
1/2 cup chopped walnuts
1/4 cup freshly grated Parmesan cheese
    Juice of 1/2 lemon
1 teaspoon salt
    Freshly ground black pepper

In a skillet sauté the zucchini in 2 tablespoons of the oil for 5 minutes, add the onion and garlic, and cook for 15 minutes. Transfer the mixture to a large heatproof bowl, add the rice, parsley, basil, and walnuts, and toss. Let the salad cool, and refrigerate.

Thirty minutes before serving, sprinkle the salad with the remaining oil, Parmesan cheese, lemon juice, and salt and pepper to taste. Toss and adjust seasonings.

Marinated Broccoli

Serves 10

1 bunch broccoli, very fresh
1 cup Vinaigrette (see "Cook's Miscellany"
    section)

Cut the broccoli into florets and marinate overnight in vinaigrette. Serve with toothpicks.

Tomatoes Stuffed with Smoked Salmon

Serves 8

8 firm ripe tomatoes
2 cucumbers, peeled, halved lengthwise
    and seeded
Salt
1/4 pound thinly sliced smoked salmon, cut
    into 1/2-inch squares
1 cup sour cream
1 tablespoon capers, drained
4 scallions, including some of the green
    tops, finely chopped
1 teaspoon finely chopped fresh dill
2 tablespoons tarragon vinegar
Freshly ground black pepper

Cut off the tops of the tomatoes and with a small spoon scoop out the insides. Invert to drain and chill.

Cut the cucumber into 1/2-inch slices, sprinkle the slices with salt, and let them stand for 30 minutes. Rinse under cold running water, drain, and dry thoroughly.

In a bowl mix the salmon with the cucumber and add the remaining ingredients. Adjust the seasonings as desired. Chill, covered, for several hours. Before serving, fill each tomato with some of the salmon mixture and garnish each with additional dill.

Fruit and Cheese with Wine

Select several cheeses with authoritative flavors, such as Roquefort, Gorgonzola, Stilton, or Asiago. For those who prefer a milder cheese, Monterey Jack, Edam, or Gouda may be added. A crock of cream cheese with walnuts is a nice addition, too.

Apples, pears, oranges, and grapes; berries, cherries, and strawberries—in season— are all appropriate. Arrange the fruits attractively in a bowl or basket and provide individual plates and fruit knives. Accompany with a pleasing, full-bodied, dry red wine.

Texas Outdoor Party

A spell of pleasant weather is all the excuse you need to invite your friends over for a casual outdoor party. Ask as few or as many people as you feel like entertaining. If the heavens open suddenly, you can crowd your guests inside; they'll understand. Or if the sun threatens to overcook your food, you can set up your serving table on a shaded porch. The Texan who planned this party likes to entertain large groups of people informally on his ranch, near San Antonio. A cool and shady unused barn makes an ideal setting for the robust menu featured here.

This party is a kind of Southwestern smorgasbord. You may want to choose just a few of these dishes. Do much of the cooking ahead of time, and plan, plan, plan. If things start to snowball, you can call for help: Caterers stand ready all the time for just such emergencies.

You can prepare the roasts ahead of time and warm them up just before the party. Cook the shrimp and mash the sweet potatoes the day before. Bake the cake early in the morning, and, of course, buy the Parker House rolls from a good baker—unless you have the time and energy to prepare them in advance for storage in the freezer (see page 114). With this kind of planning, you and your helpers have only to warm up the meats, prepare the seafood appetizers, and deep-fry the sweet potatoes before the party starts.

Oysters in Cream

Shrimp in Snow Peas

Glazed Loin of Pork   Roast Leg of Venison   Apple-Stuffed Duck

Sweet Potatoes à la Dauphine   Pasta with Red and Green Peppers

Parker House Rolls

Assorted Cheese and Crackers   Cut Fresh Fruit

Hickory Nut Cake

Oysters in Cream

Serves 12

6 dozen fresh oysters
4 1/2 cups heavy cream
1/2 pound (2 sticks) butter
Grated Parmesan cheese (optional)

Scrub oyster shells and pry open. Detach oysters from shells and remove the beards.

Preheat broiler. Return oysters to shells and add about 1 tablespoon cream to each. Dot with butter and Parmesan cheese, if you wish, and broil until edges of oysters curl.

Shrimp in Snow Peas

Serves 12

2 pounds fresh snow peas
2 1/2 pounds cooked small shrimp
1/2 cup chili sauce
2 1/2 cups catsup
3/4 cup lemon juice
3/4 cup horseradish, or more, to taste
1/2 cup Worcestershire sauce
Hot pepper sauce to taste

Trim snow peas and remove strings; carefully split each pod open along one seam. Insert 1 or 2 cooked shrimp in each snow pea.

Combine remaining ingredients and add more horseradish or pepper sauce to taste.

Arrange stuffed snow peas on serving platter; place bowl of sauce in center.

Glazed Loin of Pork

Serves 12

1 8- to 10-pound loin of pork
Salt and pepper to taste
1/3 cup Dijon mustard
1/2 cup sugar
1 jar (12 oz.) red currant jelly
1/2 cup pear nectar

Preheat oven to 500°. Rub salt and pepper over outside of pork. Place pork on rack in a large roasting pan.

Mix remaining ingredients; spoon half the mixture over pork.

Roast the pork 10 minutes at 500°. Reduce oven temperature to 350° and cook meat about 35 minutes per pound, until meat thermometer registers 185°. Baste with remaining glaze several times during cooking.

ROAST LEG OF VENISON

Serves 12

4 cups dry red wine
2 garlic cloves, crushed
1 large onion, quartered
1 leg of venison (about 7 pounds)
8 strips bacon

Combine wine, garlic, and onion. Place venison in a glass or enamel pan and pour wine mixture over it; turn meat to coat thoroughly. Marinate in the refrigerator at least 8 hours, turning occasionally. Remove meat from pan. Strain and reserve marinade.

Preheat oven to 450°. Tie venison into a manageable shape, if necessary. Place on a rack in an open roasting pan and lay the bacon strips over the top. Roast 20 minutes. Reduce oven temperature to 325° and cook 18 minutes per pound for well done; meat thermometer should register 150°. Baste with marinade several times during cooking.

APPLE-STUFFED DUCK

Serves 12

3 oven-ready ducklings (4 to 5 pounds each)
3 cooking apples, cored and quartered
1 bunch celery, cleaned and separated
2 lemons, halved
Salt

Preheat oven to 350°. Rub each duck cavity with salt and place 3 or 4 apple quarters inside each. Cut tops off celery stalks and place leaves inside ducks to fill cavities loosely. Rub outsides of ducks with cut sides of lemon; do not prick skin. Place ducks on the rack of a large roasting pan. (They should not touch; cook them separately, if necessary.) Roast 15 minutes per pound. Served duck sliced, with stuffing.

SWEET POTATOES À LA DAUPHINE

Serves 12

12 sweet potatoes, peeled and halved
Salt to taste
6 tablespoons butter
4 eggs
4 egg yolks
1/2 teaspoon nutmeg
Oil for deep-frying

Cook the potatoes in boiling salted water until softened but still firm; drain. Run through a food processor and beat until smooth. Stir in the butter, eggs, egg yolks, and nutmeg. Refrigerate several hours or overnight.

Form mixture into 1 1/2-inch balls. Deep-fry potato balls a few at a time in hot oil until warmed through and golden brown.

PASTA WITH RED AND GREEN PEPPERS

Serves 12

2 pounds short pasta or macaroni
  Salt
1 large green pepper, cored and seeded
1 large red pepper, cored and seeded
  Mayonnaise (see "Cook's Miscellany" section)
  Vinegar
2 tablespoons chopped fresh basil

Cook pasta in boiling salted water according to package directions. Drain pasta well and refresh with cold water.

Plunge peppers into lightly salted boiling water; cook 5 minutes; plunge into cold water to cool. Cut peppers into bite-sized strips.

Toss pasta with pepper strips. Thin mayonnaise slightly with a small amount of vinegar; stir into salad until pasta and pepper strips are coated. Toss in fresh basil.

HICKORY NUT CAKE

Serves 12

2/3 cup butter, softened
1²/3 cups sugar
  3 eggs
2²/3 cups flour
  2 tablespoons baking powder
1 teaspoon salt
1 teaspoon vanilla
1 cup milk
1 cup chopped hickory nuts or walnuts
  Lois's Frosting (recipe follows)

Preheat oven to 350°. Cream together butter and sugar. Beat in eggs. Sift dry ingredients together. Stir vanilla into milk. Add dry ingredients and milk to shortening, alternately and gradually. Beat until smooth. Fold in nuts. Pour batter into two greased 9-inch cake pans. Bake 25 to 30 minutes. Cool slightly. Remove from pans and cool on racks. Frost with Lois's Frosting.

LOIS'S FROSTING

Makes frosting for two-layer cake

3 tablespoons flour
1 cup milk
¹/2 pound (2 sticks) butter, softened
1 cup sugar
1 teaspoon vanilla

Whisk flour into milk over medium-low heat. Lower heat when mixture begins to thicken. Cook until thick, whisking constantly; remove from heat. Cream together butter, sugar, and vanilla until fluffy and almost white. Add cooked mixture and beat until frosting reaches the consistency of whipped cream.

St. Nicholas' Day Party

A St. Nicholas' Day celebration is a tradition originating with the early Dutch settlers and carried on by their descendants for close to three hundred years. Perhaps one of the reasons the tradition has been maintained is the opportunity the date (December 6) provides for holiday entertaining before the hustle and bustle of the full-swing holiday season.

This menu provides many Dutch holiday-time specialties, including cakes and cookies whose taste might be familiar even if the names are new to you, for they have become holiday treats for all Americans. This is especially true of Speculaas, the spiced Christmas cookies. Tea sandwiches (see Cook's Miscellany" section) are included on the menu, but it is the sweets that make this celebration a legend— not just cakes and cookies but fondant candies and marzipan, the almond-paste treats that are a Christmas tradition all over Europe. Tea and coffee are provided, as are wine punch and champagne. You'll want to have a St. Nicolas' Day party just so you can enjoy these wonderful treats—and imagine how much your guests will enjoy them. This could easily become a Christmas tradition in any house.

Kerstkrans (Christmas Ring)

Almond Cookies   Kerstkransjes (Christmas Cookies)

Gevulde Boterkoek (Buttercake with Almond Paste)

Dutch Butter Cake   Speculaas (Spiced Cookies)

Assorted Tea Sandwiches

Bowls of Fondants and Marzipan

Coffee   Tea   Champagne

KERSTKRANS (CHRISTMAS RING)

Serves 12

1 puff pastry (see "Cook's Miscellany" section)

FILLING

3/4 cup almonds, shelled, blanched, and peeled
1/4 cup granulated sugar
1 egg
1 lemon rind, grated
5 candied cherries

DECORATION

Lemon icing (recipe follows)
Apricot preserve
Red and green candied cherries, halved
Candied orange rind
Candied lemon rind, or angelica
Red ribbon
Holly

Make the filling at least one month in advance. Grind almonds finely and add sugar, egg, and grated lemon rind. Mix well. Grind

again and store almond paste in a sealed jar in the refrigerator.

Roll out puff pastry into a long strip 1/8 inch thick and 4 inches wide. Sprinkle a baking sheet with water. Find a pan cover that nearly fits the baking sheet. Put the cover in the middle of the sheet and trace the circumference (this will guide you when forming the ring). Shape almond paste into a roll of nearly the same length. Press halved candied cherries into the almond-paste roll at equal intervals so that they are not visible. Place the almond roll on dough a little above center. Wet the lower part of the dough with water and wrap loosely around almond roll. Place on a baking sheet, using the ring as a guide. Seal edges well and turn roll seam side down. Join two ends of the ring together with water. Brush with beaten egg. Allow to stand for 15 minutes in a cool place. Bake for 20 minutes in preheated 450° oven until golden brown. When baked, coat ring with a thin layer of preserve, and, while still hot, coat with lemon icing. Cool. When firm, remove from sheet and cool completely on wire rack. Decorate with candied cherries and orange and lemon rinds cut in leaf shapes. Tie red ribbon around the ring where the ends join and decorate with holly.

KERSTKRANSJES (CHRISTMAS COOKIES)

Makes about 3 dozen cookies

2 cups flour
6 tablespoons butter, softened
3/4 cup sugar
1 tablespoon milk
1 teaspoon baking powder
  Grated rind of 1/2 lemon
  Pinch of salt
1 egg, beaten
  Rock sugar
1/4 cup shelled almonds, chopped

Knead flour, butter, sugar, milk, baking powder, lemon rind, and salt into a soft ball and let stand for one hour.

Preheat oven to 350°.

Roll out sections of dough on a floured board to 1/8-inch thickness and cut out circles with a tumbler 2 1/2 inches in diameter. Place cookies on a greased baking sheet; then cut out centers with a small, round object such as a thimble. Remove centers and use them to make more cookies. Paint dough "wreaths" with beaten egg and sprinkle with a mixture of rock sugar and chopped almonds. Bake 15 to 20 minutes, until golden brown. Cool on sheet until no longer soft. Remove and cool further on a wire rack.

GEVULDE BOTERKOEK (BUTTER CAKE WITH ALMOND PASTE)

Serves 8

DOUGH

2 cups flour
1/2 pound (2 sticks) butter
1 cup superfine sugar
1 small egg
  Pinch of salt

FILLING

2 cups blanched almonds
1/4 cup sugar
1 small egg, beaten
  Grated rind of 1/2 lemon

Preheat oven to 350°.

Knead all dough ingredients into a firm ball. Divide in two and press one half into a buttered pie pan 1 inch deep and 8 inches in diameter.

Grind blanched almonds in a blender or food processor. Add sugar, egg, and lemon rind, and grind once more. Place almond paste on top of dough layer and press the other dough half on top. Bake until golden brown, about one hour. Remove from pan and cool on wire rack. Cut in wedges or diamonds.

Dutch Butter Cake

Serves 8

2¹/₂ cups sifted flour
  2 teaspoons baking powder
¹/₂ pound (2 sticks) butter, softened
1¹/₂ cups sugar
1¹/₄ teaspoons vanilla
  3 eggs, beaten

Preheat oven to 350°.

Sift flour with baking powder. Set aside. Cream butter and sugar together in a bowl and gradually add vanilla and all but 2 table-spoons egg. Add the flour mixture to the bowl and mix. Turn batter into two greased 8-inch pans. Brush tops with reserved egg. Bake for 30 minutes or until cake tester comes out clean. Cut in wedges.

Note: *Cake rises within 30 minutes and is usually done when it settles down.*

Speculaas (Spiced Cookies)

Makes about 20 squares

¹/₂ pound (2 sticks) butter, softened
1¹/₄ cups brown sugar
  1 egg
  2 teaspoons baking powder
  5 teaspoons cinnamon

  2 teaspoons ground nutmeg
  1 teaspoon ground cloves
2¹/₂ cups flour
    Blanched, slivered almonds

Preheat oven to 375°.

In a large bowl cream together butter, sugar, and egg. Mix in dry ingredients except for almonds. Put dough on a cookie sheet and roll out. Cut in squares and press slivered almonds into each square. Bake for 20 minutes.

New Year's Eve Midnight Supper

When you have decided to usher out the old year quietly, without all the whoop-de-do, noisemakers, and frantic party hopping associated with this annual institution, celebrate with an elegant, fashionably late supper with close friends. Set the mood with sparkling Christmas-tree lights, votive candles, a gay tablecloth, and a sumptuous arrangement of tulips, roses, and chincherinchee. Caterer Mark Fahrer devised a festive menu that assumes no help in the kitchen (isn't everyone partying?). Oysters on the half shell are a traditional New Year's appetizer and are treated to a delicious gourmet sauce, and duckling is prepared in a distinctly French manner. Linger over a dish of fresh fruit ices, and then ring in the New Year with a heavenly chocolate cake—and more champagne. The simplicity of the meal assures you of a relaxed, easygoing evening that your guests will remember gratefully—and may very well hope you'll repeat next year.

Oysters on the Half Shell with Mignonette Sauce
Duckling Framboise
Wild Rice   Green Beans with Almonds
Velvet Chocolate Layer Cake
Trio of Fresh Sherbets in Almond Tulip Cookies

OYSTERS ON THE HALF SHELL WITH MIGNONETTE SAUCE

Serves 4

¹/₂ cup white wine
1 tablespoon minced shallots
1 cup malt vinegar
¹/₂ cup water
1 tablespoon salt
1 tablespoon whole peppercorns, mashed
16 fresh oysters
Crushed ice
Lemon wedges
Parsley

To make the sauce, cook shallots in white wine until wine is reduced by half. Stir in the vinegar, water, salt, and peppercorns, and refrigerate one day.

Arrange 3 oysters on each plate on a bed of ice. Garnish with lemon wedges and parsley.

DUCKLING FRAMBOISE

Serves 4

Water
1 4- 4¹/₂-pound duckling
2 cups honey

FRAMBOISE SAUCE

2 cups white wine
2 shallots, minced
1 cup sugar
Juice of ¹/₂ lemon
1 cup Framboise liqueur (or 1 box frozen raspberries)
1 box fresh raspberries
Wild Rice (see "Cook's Miscellany" section)

Preheat oven to 450°. Roast the duck for 30 minutes at 450°. Remove from oven, pierce the skin here and there with a fork, and let cool 1 hour. (Carcass will separate from the skin, allowing subcutaneous fat to drip out.) Put duckling back in oven at 350° and roast until skin is crisp, about 1 hour, or 25 minutes per pound.

To make the sauce, boil wine and shallots until wine is reduced by half. In a saucepan, caramelize the sugar and lemon juice. Add wine reduction and Framboise or frozen raspberries. Puree in blender. Return to saucepan and add fresh raspberries to heat through. Carve duckling and serve slices topped with sauce. Accompany with Wild Rice.

GREEN BEANS WITH ALMONDS

Serves 4

1 pound green beans
1/4 cup slivered or sliced almonds
2 tablespoons butter
1/4 cup sliced scallions
   Salt and pepper

Steam beans until tender. In a large skillet, sauté almonds in butter until golden brown. Add scallions and cook gently until tender. Add beans and salt and pepper to taste. Toss until hot and well mixed.

VELVET CHOCOLATE LAYER CAKE

Serves 12

4 ounces unsweetened chocolate
1/2 cup water
2 1/4 cups all-purpose flour
1/2 teaspoon salt
1 teaspoon baking soda
2 sticks unsalted butter, softened
1 3/4 cups sugar
4 eggs, separated
1 teaspoon vanilla extract
1 cup milk
   Mocha Filling (recipe follows)
   Chocolate Glaze (recipe follows)
12 chocolate cigarettes

Preheat oven to 350°. Grease and flour three 9-inch round cake pans.

In a small saucepan melt chocolate and water over very low heat, stirring until smooth. Remove from heat and let cool. Sift together flour, salt, and baking soda, and set aside. Cream together butter and sugar in a large mixing bowl. Add egg yolks one at a time, beating well after each addition. Add vanilla and chocolate mixture and beat until well blended. Add sifted dry ingredients in three parts alternately with milk, beating after each addition until batter is smooth.

In a separate bowl, beat egg whites until stiff but still moist. Stir one third of egg whites into batter and fold in remainder. Divide batter evenly among cake pans. Bake 25 to 30 minutes or until toothpick or cake tester inserted in center comes out clean. Let cool in pans for 5 minutes; then turn out on racks to complete cooling. Using a bread knife, shave off rounded tops of bottom and middle cake layers. Spread tops of bottom and middle layers with mocha filling, reserving some for decoration. Place layers one atop the other and frost with chocolate glaze. Using a pastry bag, pipe reserved mocha filling around base of cake. Make 12 small drops of mocha filling on top of cake, spacing them evenly around outer edge. Rest a chocolate cigarette in each drop. Keep cake refrigerated until 15 minutes before serving.

MOCHA FILLING

1¹/₂ cups heavy whipping cream
¹/₃ cup cocoa
¹/₄ cup confectioners' sugar
2 tablespoons coffee-flavored liqueur

Place all ingredients in mixing bowl and beat at medium speed until stiff peaks form.

CHOCOLATE GLAZE

6 ounces semisweet chocolate bits
2 tablespoons butter
¹/₂ cup heavy whipping cream

In a double boiler over hot (not boiling) water, melt chocolate with butter. Remove from heat and beat in cream until smooth. Spread while warm, beginning on top of cake and moving down sides.

TRIO OF FRESH SHERBETS IN ALMOND TULIP COOKIES

1 batch Lace Cookie mix (see page 141)
1 pint mango sherbet
1 pint kiwi sherbet
1 pint lime sherbet

Preheat oven to 350°. Line a cookie sheet with parchment paper.

Allow about 2 ounces cookie dough for each cookie mold. Bake until golden brown. Remove from oven and let cool slightly. While still soft, mold into a bowl and pinch in four sides. Cool completely. Fill with a dollop of each type of sherbet.

Bridal Lunch and Shower

Such prenuptial rituals as the bridal lunch and shower can provide happy memories for years to come: a leisurely afternoon spent with your close chums in lively chitchat, hearty laughs over a shared past, opening presents earmarked for the new kitchen. This can be a welcome break from the hectic pace that precedes any wedding, large or small. A bridal shower is one of the happiest of parties to preside over. It gives you an excuse not only to bring out your nicest china and linens but to create a carefree, light menu that is as pretty to look at as it is to eat. This late-spring menu for an outdoor luncheon is designed for ease of preparation and serving. If the bride is opening packages before the lunch, you might bring out a punch bowl of mimosas—a cooling drink of half champagne and half orange juice. Those watching their waistlines would be grateful for an equally refreshing pitcher of minted iced tea. Just before serving time, arrange the prosciutto and asparagus on cold salad plates and dribble a little vinaigrette over the asparagus spears. On separate plates, unmold the rice timbales and spoon the fish salad into the tomatoes, topping each with a tablespoon of rémoulade. The assorted fruit in season may be served on a silver tray or in individual dessert plates; either way, they should be arranged in a pattern that highlights the contrasting colors. The yogurt dessert sauce is effective served in individual stemmed sherry glasses or citrus cups.

Asparagus Vinaigrette with Prosciutto
Tomatoes Stuffed with Salad of Red Snapper, Scallops, and Peaches
Wild Rice Timbales with Pine Nuts
Fresh Sliced Fruits with Raspberry Yogurt Sauce
Lace Cookies

ASPARAGUS VINAIGRETTE WITH PROSCIUTTO

Serves 8

48 asparagus spears, trimmed and
  blanched
16 slices prosciutto
  Vinaigrette (see "Cook's Miscellany"
  section)
2 Belgian endives
  Cherry tomatoes
  Fresh chives
  Chopped pimiento

Arrange asparagus in bundles of three. Wrap 1 slice of prosciutto around the middle of every three-stalk bundle. To serve, spoon 2 tablespoons vinaigrette on each salad plate and place 2 asparagus bundles on the dressing. Arrange the leaves of endive and cherry tomatoes on the side. Garnish with chopped chives and pimiento.

TOMATOES STUFFED WITH SALAD OF RED SNAPPER, SCALLOPS, AND PEACHES

Serves 8

1 bottle dry white wine
1 quart water
2 bay leaves
1 pound bay scallops
1 pound red snapper
2 ripe peaches, peeled and cut in cubes
8 whole tomatoes, skins and tops removed
  and pulp scraped out
  Rémoulade (recipe follows)
  Parsley

Put wine, water, and bay leaves into a saucepan and bring to a boil. Reduce liquid at a low boil for about 5 minutes. Lower to simmer, add scallops, and poach briefly, until tender. Be sure not to overcook. Remove scallops from stock and set aside. Poach red snapper until tender. Drain and flake.

Gently stir together scallops, snapper, and peaches. Spoon mixture into tomatoes and top with rémoulade. Garnish with parsley sprigs. Serve with Wild Rice Timbales (recipe follows).

RÉMOULADE

Makes 1 cup

1 cup Mayonnaise (see "Cook's Miscellany"
  section)
1 tablespoon Dijon mustard
2 tablespoons capers, drained and chopped
1 tablespoon fresh parsley, minced
1 tablespoon onion, finely chopped

Mix all ingredients together thoroughly and chill.

WILD RICE TIMBALES WITH PINE NUTS

Serves 8

2 cups Wild Rice (see "Cook's Miscellany" section)
1/2 cup pine nuts, toasted
Vegetable oil
Parsley

Add toasted pine nuts to cooked wild rice and mix through. Oil small molds or cups and pack with rice. Cool. Unmold alongside stuffed tomatoes. Garnish with parsley.

FRESH SLICED FRUITS WITH RASPBERRY YOGURT SAUCE

RASPBERRY SAUCE

2 boxes frozen raspberries
2 cups plain yogurt
1/2 cup Grand Marnier

FRUITS

8 lemon baskets
Fresh strawberries
Fresh pineapple, sliced
Kiwi, sliced
Blueberries
Grapes

Puree sauce ingredients in a blender. Refrigerate 1 hour.

To prepare a lemon basket, slice off a small portion of the broader end of the lemon, just enough so that it will stand upright. Then slice off top quarter or third of the lemon. Run the exposed end under hot water, to loosen pulp; then work pulp away from rind with a grapefruit knife, leaving rind intact. Scoop pulp from basket with a spoon, rinse basket gently, and pat dry.

Arrange fruits on plates with sauce for dipping in individual lemon baskets.

LACE COOKIES

1/4 cup water
1/4 cup white liquid corn sugar
3/4 cup brown sugar
4 tablespoons butter, melted until it boils
2 tablespoons flour
1 cup blanched slivered almonds

Preheat oven to 350°. Grease 2 baking sheets.

Beat together water, glucose, sugar, and butter. Add flour and almonds to cookie mixture and mix thoroughly. Place 1-inch dollops of batter 3 inches apart on baking sheet and bake until golden brown, about 5 minutes.

No-Kitchen Party

Some of the best parties take place far from the kitchen. At a tailgate picnic or a roof-raising party, for example, the nearest stove could be miles away. And at an office party or a beach gathering, there won't be a kitchen anywhere in sight. But that small inconvenience doesn't stop determined party givers. They simply choose foods that travel well; then they prepare everything ahead of time, tote it all away in cooling chests, and join the fun.

The menu on these pages, which was made up for a fairly large party, has as its main dish a cold pasta with chicken and colorful garnishes. This dish is not difficult to prepare, but you'll be making large quantities of everything, so give yourself plenty of time. You'll need only one very large pot if you keep washing and reusing it while the earlier batches of chicken and pasta cool in the refrigerator.

A light dessert is usually welcome after a filling pasta. If other easy-to-handle fruits are in season when you throw your far-out party, you may want to serve them instead of grapes and cherries. You can prepare the brownies a day ahead and refrigerate them until party time, or you may prefer to buy assorted cookies from the best bakery in town.

Iced Tea, Soft Drinks, Wine and Beer
Cucumber Sticks, Scallions, and Snow Peas with Lemon Anchovy Dip
Assorted Chips and Crackers
Cold Pasta and Chicken Supreme with Vegetable Garnishes
Tossed Salad with Italian Dressing
Pita Rounds and French Bread with Poppy Seed Butter and Herb Butter
Fresh Grapes and Cherries
No-Bake Brownies

LEMON ANCHOVY DIP

Makes 6 cups

5 lemons
10 egg yolks
1 cup Dijon mustard
5 cans (2 ounces each) anchovy fillets, undrained
5 shallots, chopped
5 cups vegetable oil
Salt and pepper to taste

Squeeze lemons, reserving juice. Put egg yolks, mustard, anchovies with their liquid, lemon juice, and shallots in a blender or food processor and mix until foamy. Add oil very slowly while processor is running, stopping it occasionally to make sure oil is blending with egg mixture. Add salt and pepper to taste. Refrigerate.

COLD PASTA AND CHICKEN SUPREME WITH VEGETABLE GARNISHES

Serves 40

2¹/₂ pounds small pasta such as shells, bow ties, or wheels
5 cups Garlic Mustard Dressing (recipe follows)
7 chickens (3 pounds each), cooked in broth (recipe follows)
5 cups mayonnaise
2¹/₂ pounds mushrooms
3 garlic cloves, quartered
¹/₂ cup lemon juice
²/₃ cup chicken broth
¹/₂ cup olive oil
5 packages (9 ounces each) frozen artichoke hearts
5 avocados, peeled, pitted, and cut into wedges
5 pints cherry tomatoes
6 bunches scallions, chopped
1 bunch fresh parsley or watercress, chopped

Cook pasta about 1 pound at a time, according to package directions. Drain well; place in large bowls. Pour about 2 cups Garlic Mustard Dressing over warm pasta and toss well. Cover and refrigerate several hours. Skin, bone, and cut up cooked chicken; mix into pasta. Add mayonnaise and toss to blend. Refrigerate.

Cook mushrooms, whole or sliced, with garlic cloves in lemon juice, olive oil, and chicken broth, about 8 minutes. Refrigerate.

Cook artichoke hearts according to package directions. Refrigerate.

Mound pasta on serving plates. Arrange mushrooms on top. Place artichoke hearts and avocado wedges in separate bowls; add remaining salad dressing to each bowl and stir to coat. Arrange tomatoes, artichokes, and avocados around pasta. Sprinkle with scallions and parsley.

GARLIC MUSTARD DRESSING
Makes 7¹/₂ cups

1¹/₂ cups wine vinegar
4 tablespoons Dijon mustard
1 tablespoon minced garlic
Salt and pepper to taste
1¹/₂ cups olive oil
4¹/₂ cups vegetable oil

Combine vinegar, mustard, garlic, salt, and pepper in a blender. Add oil a little at a time, processing as you do so. Mix again before serving.

CHICKEN COOKED IN BROTH
Serves 4–6

1 fryer chicken (about 3 pounds)
Water to cover chicken
1 bay leaf
3 sprigs fresh parsley
¹/₂ cup chopped celery
1 onion stuck with 2 cloves
1 carrot, trimmed and scraped

Place all ingredients in a large kettle. Bring to a boil, reduce heat, and simmer, covered, 50 minutes or until tender.

ITALIAN DRESSING
Makes 5 cups

2 cups olive oil
2 cups vegetable oil
1 cup red wine vinegar
2 teaspoons salt
¹/₂ teaspoon pepper
3 garlic cloves, peeled and quartered

Mix the oils, vinegar, salt, and pepper. Trim and peel garlic cloves and add to dressing. Refrigerate at least 24 hours or as long as 2 days. Remove garlic before serving.

POPPY SEED BUTTER
Serves 40

1¹/₄ pounds (5 sticks) butter
¹/₂ cup poppy seeds
40 small pita rounds

Let butter soften at room temperature. Stir in poppy seeds and press butter into a serving dish. Cover and refrigerate. Serve with pita bread.

HERB BUTTER
Serves 40

1¹/₄ pounds (5 sticks) butter
¹/₂ cup chopped parsley
¹/₂ cup chopped chives
¹/₄ cup chopped basil
5 loaves French bread

Let butter soften at room temperature. Blend in remaining ingredients. Press butter into serving dish. Cover and refrigerate. Serve with French bread.

NO-BAKE BROWNIES

Makes 64 squares

4 12-ounce packages semisweet chocolate
  bits
1 pound sweet butter
10 cups graham cracker crumbs
4 cups walnuts, chopped
4 14-ounce cans condensed milk
4 teaspoons vanilla

In the top of a double boiler melt the chocolate with the butter and stir until smooth. Combine the remaining ingredients in a bowl; then stir in the chocolate mixture. (The batter will be very thick.) Pat the batter evenly into four 8- or 9-inch-square baking pans. Let stand at room temperature for several hours; cut brownies into squares and seal each with plastic wrap.

Marin County Supper

One debate this menu might provoke at the dinner table is the question of which California phe-nomenon has had more impact on '80s life-styles, Silicon Valley technology or lean cuisine? A persuasive case can be made for the latter, since these are dishes representing cooking at its tastiest, prettiest, healthiest, and easiest. Whether you make this a quick and easy dinner for six or multiply the ingredi-ents to form a light al fresco *buffet supper for a crowd, it is a striking medley of flavors and colors, one that is hard to beat for ease of preparation and service. Those watching their waistline will be grateful for a meal they can enjoy without guilt. If the dessert proves to be irresistible, never mind; the total calorie count is probably half that of the average three-course traditional meal. A sleight-of-hand learned from some of the world's most famous health spas: small portions served artistically so that the food is a feast wholly satisfying to the eye (tricking the stomach into believing it has not been deprived). For the cook, it is the ease of preparation that is tempting. And for those pressed for time, a carrot cake will not be looked down on if ordered from a bakery. Complete the California look with bright napkins and flowers and a chilled California white such as a chardonnay.*

Scallop Ceviche
Caesar Salad
Chicken Gismonda
Sesame Asparagus
Herbed French Bread
Carrot Cake with Cream Cheese Frosting

Scallop Ceviche

Serves 6

1 1/2 pounds fresh bay scallops
1 cup fresh lemon juice or fresh lime
    juice
1/4 cup chopped scallions
1 small can green chilies, chopped
10 cherry tomatoes, cut in half
1/4 cup olive oil
2 tablespoons chopped parsley
Salt and freshly ground black pepper

In a bowl marinate the scallops in the lemon or lime juice for 3 or 4 hours. Drain. Add the remaining ingredients and toss. Season to taste. Let stand at least 1 more hour. Serve in scallop shells or on lettuce leaves.

Note: *If using sea scallops, slice them 1/4 inch thick.*

Variations: *Ceviche can be made with any white fish cut into 1-inch cubes or with a combination of scallops and other fish.*

Caesar Salad

Serves 6

1 head romaine lettuce, washed and
    torn into pieces
1/3 cup olive oil
2 cloves garlic, finely minced
3 tablespoons lemon juice
Salt

Pepper
1 egg, coddled (simmered 2 minutes)
3–4 anchovy fillets
1/4 cup grated Parmesan cheese
1 cup garlic croutons

Arrange lettuce in a large wooden bowl. Add olive oil and toss. Add garlic, lemon juice, salt, and pepper, and toss lightly. Break egg onto salad and add anchovies. Toss gently. Sprinkle with cheese and croutons. Toss just before serving.

Chicken Gismonda

Serves 6

3 whole chicken breasts, boned and split
Salt
Pepper
Bread crumbs
5 tablespoons butter
1 1/2 pounds spinach, thoroughly washed
    and stemmed
3/4 pound mushrooms, thinly sliced
5 tablespoons cream
4 tablespoons finely chopped parsley

Season chicken with salt and pepper. Dredge in bread crumbs, knocking off excess. Melt half of the butter in a skillet. Sauté the

PUREE OF APPLE SOUP

Serves 8

4 tablespoons butter
1 small onion, finely chopped
6–7 apples, unpeeled, cored, and sliced
    Salt and freshly ground white pepper
4 cups beef broth
4 tablespoons dry sherry
1¼ teaspoons arrowroot, mixed with 1
    tablespoon water
⅓ cup blanched, slivered almonds,
    sautéed in 2 teaspoons butter

In a large saucepan, melt the butter and cook the onion until golden. Add apple slices and salt and pepper to taste, and cook the mixture until apples are tender. Add broth and sherry, bring to a boil, and simmer for 15 minutes. Stir in arrowroot mixture and cook soup, stirring, until thickened. Adjust seasonings. Strain soup through a fine sieve into another pan and reheat it. Serve the soup in warmed bowls and sprinkle with almonds.

PRUNE-STUFFED PORK WITH ROASTED POTATOES AND CARROTS

Serves 8

1 boneless loin of pork (3½ pounds) with
    the bones reserved
16 pitted prunes (if not moist, soak for 1
    hour in hot tea)
    Salt and freshly ground black pepper
2¼ pounds tiny new potatoes, scrubbed, or
    medium-size regular potatoes, peeled
    and quartered
2 pounds baby carrots, scrubbed, or regu-
    lar carrots, peeled, halved, then
    quartered lengthwise
4 tablespoons vegetable oil
½ cup Madeira
½ cup water
1 tablespoon arrowroot mixed with
    ¼ cup water

Preheat the oven to 375°.

Using a knife with a long, thin blade, run it through the middle of the pork loin (lengthwise) to make a pocket for the prunes. (You may have to do this from each end rather than in one stroke.) Drain prunes and insert them into the pocket with your fingers. Tie pork with a string to retain its shape and keep the pocket closed. Season with salt and pepper.

Put the pork in a shallow roasting pan, fat side up, and surround it with reserved bones. Roast for 2 hours, turning every 15 minutes.

One hour before roast will be done, place the potatoes and carrots in a baking pan and drizzle with oil. Place beside the roast and baste occasionally with pork drippings. Keep warm while making pork gravy.

When roast is done, remove to a platter and keep warm. Discard bones, pour off fat, and add wine and water to the brown bits that have collected in the pan. Bring to a boil and add salt and pepper to taste if needed. Strain gravy and thicken with arrowroot mixture. Slice pork and serve with gravy.

PECAN PIE

Serves 8

1 9-inch Plain Tart Crust (see "Cook's
    Miscellany" section)
3/4 cup sugar
1 tablespoon flour
1/4 teaspoon salt
3/4 cup light corn syrup
4 eggs, lightly beaten
1/4 cup butter, melted
2 cups pecan halves
6 ounces semisweet chocolate pieces
1/3 cup heavy cream
    Sweetened whipped cream

Refrigerate pie shell until filling is ready.
Preheat oven to 350°.

In a large bowl, combine sugar, flour,
and salt. Stir in corn syrup, eggs, and butter.
Add the pecans and pour mixture into the
prepared pie shell. Bake for 55 minutes, or
until set. Remove the pie from the oven and
place on a wire rack to cool. In a small saucepan, over low heat, melt chocolate pieces with
the cream. Stir to combine; then spread chocolate mixture over the top of the cooled pie.
Serve the pie chilled, topped with sweetened
whipped cream.

Dog River al Fresco Buffet

What better way to spend an evening during the hazy, lazy dog days of August than over a casual, informal meal among family and friends. Relaxed hospitality prevails at this evening buffet on the banks of Dog River outside Mobile, Alabama.

Legend has it that the early French settlers readily adapted to the leisurely pace of the Indians and nicknamed their ambling Red River La Rive du chien, *or Dog River. The Deep South has cultivated the art of taking it easy ever since.*

The West Indies Salad featured here is a deceptively simple concoction of crabmeat marinated in a vinaigrette dressing and served on lettuce leaves in scallop shells—a cooling prelude to the crowd-pleasing, heartier fare of roast pork and traditional Southern side dishes. At meal's end, protestations aside, no one will be able to resist a slice of freshly baked pecan pie.

West Indies Salad with Crabmeat

Roast Pork

Stuffed Tomatoes   **Garlic Grits**   **Fried Okra**

Cucumber Mold

Corn Sticks

Pecan Pie

WEST INDIES SALAD WITH CRABMEAT

Serves 8

1 cup salad oil
1/3 cup cider vinegar
1/2 teaspoon salt
1 teaspoon dry mustard
1/4 teaspoon pepper
2 tablespoons chopped capers
2 teaspoons chopped chives
4 cups cooked crabmeat, shredded
   Lettuce leaves

Combine first 7 ingredients and blend well. Pour over crabmeat and refrigerate until serving time. Serve on lettuce leaves.

ROAST PORK

1 6- to 7-pound pork loin   Serves 8
   Dijon mustard
   Salt and pepper to taste
1/4 cup all-purpose flour

Preheat oven to 450°. Place roast on the rack of a roasting pan and spread mustard over entire surface. Season with salt and pepper. Sift a thin coating of flour over roast. Bake at 450° for 45 minutes. Reduce oven temperature to 350° and bake 35 to 45 minutes per pound (185° on meat thermometer).

STUFFED TOMATOES

Serves 8

8 ripe, meaty tomatoes
8 strips bacon
1 onion, chopped
2 cups croutons
1 1/4 cups brown sugar
   Salt and pepper to taste

Preheat oven to 325°. Core tomatoes and scoop out centers to form cups; chop pulp and set aside. Cook bacon; crumble and set aside. Cook onion in bacon drippings until wilted but not browned; drain. Mix onion, tomato pulp, croutons, half the brown sugar, crumbled bacon, salt, and pepper. Fill tomato cups with the mixture. Sprinkle remaining brown sugar on top of stuffing. Bake 15 to 20 minutes, until sugar bubbles.

GARLIC GRITS

Serves 8

2 cups grits
1/4 pound (1 stick) butter
3 tablespoons Worcestershire sauce
1 pound sharp Cheddar cheese, grated
1 clove garlic, minced
   Hot pepper sauce to taste
4 egg whites

Cook grits according to package directions.
Preheat oven to 400°. To hot grits add all ingredients except egg whites and stir well. Cool slightly. Beat egg whites until soft peaks form. Fold into mixture and pour into large, greased baking dish. Bake 20 minutes.

FRIED OKRA

Serves 8

3–4 cups fresh okra, sliced into rounds
1 1/2 quarts boiling water
   1 cup cornmeal
      Salt and pepper to taste
   3 tablespoons shortening
   1 tablespoon bacon drippings

Drop okra into boiling water and cook 5 minutes; drain on paper towels. Combine cornmeal, salt, and pepper in a paper or plastic bag. Shake okra, about 1 cup at a time, in cornmeal mixture to coat. In a heavy skillet, heat shortening and bacon drippings. Cook okra in hot fat about 1 cup at a time, avoiding overcrowding, until golden brown.

CUCUMBER MOLD

Serves 8

   3 tablespoons unflavored gelatin
   2 cups water
1/2 cup chopped onion
1/2 cup chopped celery
1/4 cup white vinegar
   1 tablespoon tarragon vinegar
   3 tablespoons sugar
   1 teaspoon salt
      Red pepper to taste
1/2 teaspoon Worcestershire sauce
   2 garlic cloves, crushed
   3 medium cucumbers, peeled and grated
1/2 cup heavy cream
3–4 drops green food coloring (optional)
1/2 cup mayonnaise

Soften gelatin in 1/4 cup water. Bring 1/2 cup water to a boil. Drop in chopped onion and cook 3 minutes; drain. Bring another 1/2 cup water to a boil; cook celery 5 minutes; drain. Mix together white and tarragon vinegars, remaining 3/4 cup water, sugar, salt, red pepper, Worcestershire sauce, onion, and garlic. Heat 1 cup vinegar-onion mixture almost to boiling; remove from heat and stir in gelatin. Add remaining vinegar-onion mixture; blend thoroughly and allow to cool 10 to 15 minutes. Stir celery and cucumbers into cooled mixture. Refrigerate until partially set.

Whip heavy cream, adding food coloring if you wish, and fold whipped cream into mayonnaise; add to cucumber mixture, stirring gently to blend. Rinse 1-quart ring mold with cold water and, leaving it wet, fill with cucumber mixture. Refrigerate 4 hours or overnight. Unmold on a serving dish.

CORN STICKS

Serves 8 to 12

   1 cup all-purpose flour
   2 teaspoons baking powder
   2 tablespoons sugar
3/4 teaspoon salt
1/2 teaspoon baking soda
   1 cup yellow cornmeal
   1 egg
3/4 cup whole milk or buttermilk
1/4 cup liquid shortening

Preheat oven to 425°. Grease an iron corn-stick pan and place in oven to heat. Sift together flour, baking powder, sugar, salt, and baking soda. Stir in cornmeal. Add egg, milk, and shortening. Beat with spoon only until well mixed. Pour into hot corn-stick molds, filling about ⅔ full. Bake until golden, 12 to 15 minutes.

PECAN PIE

Serves 8

1 9-inch Plain Tart Crust (see "Cook's
    Miscellany" section)
2 cups pecan halves
3 eggs
⅛ teaspoon salt
¾ cup sugar
1 cup dark corn syrup
¼ pound (1 stick) butter, melted
½ teaspoon vanilla extract

Preheat oven to 350°. Chop about ¼ cup pecans and spread over bottom of pie shell. With wooden spoon, beat eggs with salt until mixture thickens. Gradually beat in sugar. Add corn syrup, melted butter, and vanilla; stir well. Pour into pie shell. Spread remaining pecans on top. Bake 1 hour.

Romantic Dinner for Two

Valentine's Day, of course, is the perfect time for a frankly seductive dinner. (So is the third Tuesday in August for that matter. Or maybe you just got a promotion; your lover is back from an extended business trip; all of the kids are away for the weekend; you can't wait to show off that flattering caftan.) . . . Mark Fahrer, a cosmopolitan and gourmet, came up with a menu prescribed to melt the heart of even the most intransigent of innamorati: meat and potatoes, with panache!

On a night like this, tuck away all those acquired skills of subtlety and subterfuge and greet him or her with a bucket of champagne on ice, a perfectly set table, candlelight, soft music, and helium-filled balloons (if you feel you need to drive home the point).

With the exception of the Tournedos Périgueux, everything may be prepared ahead and kept waiting up to the last moment before serving—for who can predict what time you'll want to serve dinner when the evening is designed for love?

Heart-Shaped Puff Pastry Filled with Asparagus
Tournedos with Sauce Périgueux
Potatoes Anna
Snow Peas
Mocha Soufflé

HEART-SHAPED PUFF PASTRY FILLED WITH ASPARAGUS

Serves 2

1 sheet Puff Pastry (see "Cook's Miscellany" section)
8–10 spears asparagus, trimmed and blanched

BEURRE BLANC
2 tablespoons minced shallots
3/4 cup white wine
1 cup heavy cream
4 tablespoons butter

Cut puff pastry dough into 2 heart-shaped pieces. Bake at 350° until golden brown.

To make the *beurre blanc*, boil shallots in wine until nearly all the wine is evaporated. Lower heat and add butter, in 3 or 4 pieces, whisking into sauce as you do so. When butter is smooth, add heavy cream and simmer to reduce until slightly thickened. Do not let boil. Serve asparagus on puff pastry shells.

TOURNEDOS WITH SAUCE PÉRIGUEUX

Serves 2

SAUCE PÉRIGUEUX
1 tablespoon unsalted butter
1 large shallot, finely chopped
1/2 cup dry red wine
5 ounces beef bouillon
Pinch of thyme
2 tablespoons butter, softened
2 tablespoons flour
1/4 cup Madeira
2 tablespoons finely chopped black truffle
Salt and freshly ground black pepper

TOURNEDOS:
2 1/4-pound beef fillets wrapped in pork fat
2 tablespoons butter
Salt and pepper
Watercress

The sauce may be prepared in advance up to the addition of the Madeira. Melt the butter in a heavy saucepan and sauté the shallots over medium heat until limp and golden. Stir in the wine and bouillon and bring to a boil. Season with thyme and cook sauce until reduced by half. Work the butter and flour into a paste to make a beurre manié. Make into little balls and drop one at a time into reduced sauce, whisking constantly. Cook until sauce reaches desired thickness. Put through a strainer to remove bits of shallot. (Sauce may be refrigerated at this time, or set aside while tournedos are cooked.)

To prepare the tournedos, heat the butter in a heavy skillet, until the foam starts to subside, indicating that it is hot enough to sear the steaks. Season steaks with salt and pepper and sauté 3 to 4 minutes on each side. Transfer to a heated platter and keep warm.

Pour off the fat from the skillet. Add the sauce and the Madeira. Bring to a boil, then turn down and simmer until reduced to ½ cup. Stir in the chopped truffles. Season to taste. Remove pork fat from fillets. Spoon sauce over tournedos or serve on individual plates.

POTATOES ANNA

Serves 2

2 baking potatoes, peeled and thinly sliced
½ cup chicken stock
¼ cup grated Parmesan cheese
2 tablespoons butter

Arrange potato slices in a small baking or soufflé dish. Pour chicken stock over potatoes. Bake for 30 minutes at 350°. Drain off excess stock. Sprinkle with grated Parmesan cheese, dot with butter, and brown top in broiler.

SNOW PEAS

½ pound snow peas
½ quart water
1 tablespoon butter
Salt and pepper

Bring water to a boil. Add snow peas and cook for 1 minute. Drain and refresh peas in cold water. Before serving, heat butter in a skillet till quite hot but not sizzling, add snow peas, and sauté briefly. Add salt and pepper and serve immediately.

FROZEN MOCHA SOUFFLÉ

4 egg yolks
½ cup sugar
2 tablespoons instant espresso coffee
2 squares (2 ounces) unsweetened chocolate
2 tablespoons water
2 tablespoons rum or cognac
1 cup heavy cream, whipped
Chocolate shavings

Beat egg yolks, sugar, and instant coffee until thick and creamy. In a small saucepan, melt chocolate with water; add rum and stir into egg and coffee mixture. Fold whipped cream into soufflé. Pour into dessert glasses or a two-cup soufflé dish and freeze overnight. Decorate with chocolate shavings.

A Cocktail Buffet

Here are seven delicious hors-d'oeuvres recipes, as diverse in flavor as they are in color and presentation. Though they might appear complicated enough to lead to disaster, they're not; again, it is a matter of preparing several of these tasty dishes ahead of time. Both the cannelloni and the mushroom croustades can be made and then frozen until ready for use. The cheese straws and souffléed crackers can also be made beforehand and stored in plastic bags or some other airtight container. Though the monkfish and cherry tomatoes must be prepared the day of the event, they can both be made early on, and then chilled, as can the spinach dip and the avocado filling for the tomatoes. If you hire help, or just have a few extra hands in the kitchen, the final assembly of each item and of the buffet table will take no time at all, giving you those necessary pre-party hours to relax and dress.

Cannelloni
Spinach Dip with Vegetables
Mushroom Croustades
Cheese Straws
Monkfish with Spiced Mayonnaise
Souffléed Saltines
Cherry Tomatoes Stuffed with Avocado

CANNELLONI

Serves 20

MORNAY SAUCE

6 tablespoons butter
6 tablespoons flour
4 cups milk, heated
1 bay leaf
1½ cups grated Swiss cheese
½ teaspoon nutmeg
 Salt

Melt butter and stir in the flour. Whisk 2 to 3 minutes over medium-low heat to cook the flour. Gradually add milk, continuing to whisk until sauce comes to a boil. Add bay leaf and simmer until sauce is thick and smooth. Remove from heat, take out bay leaf, and stir in cheese, nutmeg, and salt to taste. Mix until smooth. Reserve, covered, over barely simmering water.

TOMATO SAUCE

6 tablespoons olive oil
2 medium onions, chopped
2 celery stalks, finely chopped
2 small carrots, scraped and finely
 chopped
3 cloves garlic, crushed
5 8-ounce cans plum tomatoes, chopped,
 with juice
4 tablespoons tomato paste
2 tablespoons chopped fresh basil
1 teaspoon marjoram

½ cup chopped fresh parsley
 Salt and freshly ground pepper

Heat the oil in a large, non-aluminum skillet; add onion, celery, and carrots, and cook slowly, until vegetable mixture is soft. Add garlic, tomatoes, tomato paste, basil, marjoram, and parsley. Simmer, partly covered, over low heat, for about 45 minutes, or until sauce is thick. Stir frequently. Season to taste with salt and pepper.

FILLING

6 tablespoons olive oil
2 medium onions, finely chopped
2 carrots, finely chopped
2 cloves garlic, minced
3 pounds lean ground beef
2 pounds ground veal
1½ cups dry white wine
2 10-ounce packages frozen spinach,
 thawed and drained
5 eggs, beaten
2 teaspoons salt
1 teaspoon nutmeg

½ cup parsley, finely chopped
  Freshly ground pepper
1 cup Mornay sauce
  Manicotti shells, pasta tubes, or crêpes

Heat oil in a large skillet and sauté onion and carrot until onion is translucent. Add garlic for one minute and then transfer ingredients to large bowl. Add meat to the skillet and cook until no longer pink; then add wine and simmer for 20 minutes. Remove from heat and stir in drained spinach. Put mixture with liquid in a blender or food processor to blend. Process about 2 cups of the mixture at a time, transferring each batch to a large bowl. When all the meat is blended, add the eggs, salt, nutmeg, parsley, and Mornay sauce. Mix ingredients thoroughly and set aside.

To assemble, cover the bottom of two long, flat baking dishes with a layer of tomato sauce and set aside. Place 2 to 3 tablespoons of the meat filling at the center of each pasta tube and spread the mixture in a straight line. Roll up and layer in the baking dishes. Pour the remaining Mornay sauce over the cannelloni, spreading it evenly. Then spoon tomato sauce over each dish, making 2 separate bands running lengthwise.

Heat oven to 350°. Bake for 25 minutes or until the sauce is bubbly at the edges of the pan. Just before serving, put the cannelloni under the broiler for a minute or two to brown the top.

SPINACH DIP
Makes 2½ cups

1 8-ounce package cream cheese
1 cup sour cream
½ cup Mayonnaise (see "Cook's Miscellany" section)
1 envelope leek-soup mix
1 small clove garlic, crushed
  Pinch of dried dill weed
1 10-ounce package frozen chopped spinach, thawed, drained, and squeezed dry
  Small head red cabbage

In the bowl of a food processor, combine the cream cheese and sour cream and blend well. Add mayonnaise, soup mix, and seasonings. Process until well blended. Gently stir in spinach. Serve with assorted vegetables.

MUSHROOM CROUSTADES

Makes 2 to 3 dozen

1 pound Puff Pastry (see "Cook's
    Miscellany" section)
3 tablespoons butter
1 large onion, finely chopped
1 pound mushrooms, chopped
1/4 teaspoon thyme
1/2 teaspoon salt
    Dash of pepper
2 tablespoons flour
2/3 cup sour cream
1 tablespoon sherry

Roll out pastry. Shape and mold into tartlet pans. Place pans on a baking sheet and refrigerate. Heat butter; sauté onion; add mushrooms, and cook 3 minutes. Add seasonings; sprinkle in flour, and mix to blend. Stir in sour cream. Cook until thick but not boiling. Remove from heat and add sherry.

Preheat oven to 400°.

Fill pastry shells (about 1 teaspoon per tart); bake 20 minutes. Serve hot.

Note: *Tarts can be frozen before baking. If frozen, bake at 350° for 30 minutes.*

CHEESE STRAWS

Makes 5 dozen

2 cups flour
1/2 teaspoon salt
4 tablespoons butter
1 cup Gruyère cheese, freshly grated
1 cup Parmesan cheese, freshly grated

Preheat the oven to 350°.

In a bowl, combine all the ingredients and mix well. Roll out as you would pastry and cut into 3-inch strips. Bake until golden, about 8 to 10 minutes. The straws may be frozen or stored in a tightly covered container.

Note: *You can use leftover bits of other cheeses in this recipe.*

MONKFISH WITH SPICED MAYONNAISE

Makes 40–50 pieces

3–4 monkfish fillets, skinned, or about 2 1/2
    pounds
3 cups Fish Stock or court-bouillon
    (recipe follows)
Salt
White pepper
3 scallions
1 cup Spiced Mayonnaise (recipe follows)
2 dozen cherry tomatoes
3 limes, quartered

Cut fillets in half crosswise and arrange them skin side down in the bottom of a large saucepan or deep-sided skillet. Fillets should not overlap one another. If necessary, use two pans, or poach in stages.

Add just enough stock or *court-bouillon* to cover fillets. (If necessary, add 1 part wine to 2 parts water to liquid until fish is barely covered.) Bring stock to the boil and lower immediately to simmer. Poach fillets till done, about 10 to 15 minutes, depending on thickness of fillets. Fillets are done when uniform in color and easily pierced with a fork.

Remove fillets from pan, taking care to keep them intact, and set aside. When fillets are cool enough to handle, cut into cubes of about 1½ inches, or slightly larger than bite-size. Sprinkle lightly with salt and white pepper, toss gently, and refrigerate, covered.

Trim ends off scallions and cut crosswise in half. Slice halved scallions lengthwise into juliennes or shreds.

To serve, bring monkfish pieces to room temperature or slightly cooler. Place a cup-size bowl or ramekin of spiced mayonnaise at the center of a serving platter, and scatter fish around the center, interspersed with whole cherry tomatoes. Skewer each fish piece and tomato with a decorated toothpick and scatter scallion shreds loosely over all. Line edges of platter with quartered limes.

FISH STOCK

Makes 3 cups

Bones and head of 1 fish
1 tablespoon butter
1 tablespoon olive oil

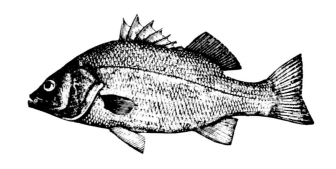

1 medium onion, coarsely chopped
1 clove garlic, crushed
1 large carrot, quartered
2 stalks celery, quartered, with tops
1 bay leaf
2 sprigs thyme, or 1 teaspoon dried
2 cups dry vermouth or white wine
3 cups water

In a saucepan, brown fish head and bones in butter and oil over medium-high heat. Add onion, garlic, carrots, and celery, and cook, stirring, till softened, about 4 or 5 minutes. Toss in bay leaves and thyme, turn up flame, and add wine. Cook at a high boil for 1 or 2 minutes, add water, return to the boil, and lower to simmer.

Simmer stock, covered, for 30 minutes. (Let simmer longer for richer stock, adding a little water and wine occasionally as liquid evaporates.) Strain stock to reserve, pressing down on solids in the strainer to extract all the juices.

Note: *If you do not have fish parts, follow procedures for remaining ingredients to make a* court-bouillon.

SPICED MAYONNAISE

Makes 1 cup

1 cup Mayonnaise (see "Cook's Miscellany"
    section)
1 tablespoon Fish Stock
1 tablespoon fresh lime juice
1 teaspoon prepared horseradish, drained
1 teaspoon dried capers, chopped or crushed
4 cornichons, or 1 or 2 sour gherkins, finely
    chopped

Put prepared mayonnaise in a blender, add fish stock and lime juice, and process to blend and re-thicken. Transfer to a mixing bowl; add horseradish, capers, and chopped pickle; and blend thoroughly.

SOUFFLÉED SALTINES

36 saltine crackers
    Water
¼ pound (1 stick) butter, softened

Soak the crackers in cold water for 20 minutes. Lift them out with a slotted spatula and drain.

Preheat the oven to 400°.

Place the crackers 1½ inches apart on cookie sheets, dot the tops with butter, and bake for ½ hour. *Do not open the oven door.* The crackers may be stored in an airtight container.

CHERRY TOMATOES STUFFED WITH AVOCADO

Serves 20

4 pints cherry tomatoes
    Salt
    Sugar
4 medium avocados
4 tablespoons heavy cream
4 tablespoons finely chopped parsley
6 teaspoons fresh lime juice
3 teaspoons fresh lemon juice
3 teapoons finely chopped fresh chives
    Hot pepper sauce to taste
    Salad greens
    Watercress leaves

Cut a thin slice from the top of each cherry tomato and scoop out the flesh and seeds with a melon-ball cutter. Discard the tops of the tomatoes. Sprinkle the insides with salt and sugar, invert the tomatoes on paper towels, and let them drain for 40 minutes.

Cut each avocado in half lengthwise, scoop out the pulp, and mash it in a bowl. Add the remaining ingredients, except the greens, and mix well. Divide the filling among the tomatoes. Serve on a platter of salad greens garnished with watercress.

TV Dinner

Here is a tasty, well-rounded meal for one of those evenings when you just don't feel like spending time in the kitchen. Each item on the menu can be easily prepared. The pot pie, contributed by Lynne Bien of New York's Pie in the Sky, requires a bit more time to assemble than the other elements but can be made ahead of time, frozen, then thawed and reheated in a matter of minutes. The Oreo Ice Cream should be made beforehand, too, as it must be frozen. Both the chicken pies and the oreo ice cream will be particularly popular with children, though the meal is just as appropriate for a cosy midweek repast for two. So get into your most comfortable clothes, switch on the TV, and enjoy with each other, the family or a group of friends.

Chicken Pot Pie
Green Bean Salad
Oreo Ice Cream

CHICKEN POT PIE

Serves 4

2 boneless, skinless chicken breasts
3 cups chicken broth
1 cup white wine
2 sprigs parsley
1 celery top
  Pinch of thyme
¾ cup carrots
¾ cup potatoes, lightly cooked
¾ cup celery
½ cup cut string beans, peas or zucchini
  Sauce Velouté (recipe follows)
  Salt, pepper, and onion powder to taste
  Pot-Pie Crust (recipe follows)

Preheat oven to 400°.

Poach chicken breasts in broth and white wine with parsley sprigs, celery tops, and a pinch of thyme. When chicken is tender, drain, and cut in bite-size pieces. Arrange pieces in bottoms of 4 individual pot-pie dishes and distribute vegetables on top. Fill to the top of dish with velouté. Season to taste with salt, pepper, and a little powdered onion. Follow directions listed in crust recipe and bake for 20 minutes, or until crust is brown.

SAUCE VELOUTÉ

4 tablespoons butter or chicken fat
4 tablespoons flour
6 cups chicken stock

Melt butter, stir in flour until smooth, and cook the roux slowly for 5 or 6 minutes without browning. Gradually whisk in strained stock and cook until thickened and smooth. Adjust seasonings and add more or less liquid according to your own taste, but remember that it will continue to thicken as it bakes in the pies.

POT-PIE CRUST

2 cups all-purpose flour
½ teaspoon salt
8 ounces (2 sticks) unsalted butter, chilled
¼ cup ice water
1 egg
1 tablespoon cream

Process flour, salt, and butter in the bowl of a food processor until it resembles coarse meal. Add water by drops, turning food processor on and off. Do not overprocess. When dough forms a ball, remove and chill for 1 hour.

Divide pastry in half and roll out one half to ⅛-inch thickness on a lightly floured board. Cut rolled half into four equal sections, allowing each to drape over the edge of its pie dish. Add filling and sauce. Roll out other half and divide. Place sections over filled pies and cut vents in each. Trim excess dough around edges, leaving a slight overhang. Fold bottom overhangs over tops of each and crimp to seal. Beat egg and cream together and glaze.

GREEN BEAN SALAD

Serves 4

1½ pounds young green beans
½ pound large white mushrooms
½ cup walnut halves
Salt and freshly ground pepper
¼ cup fresh lemon juice
½ cup walnut oil

In a saucepan cook the beans, uncovered, in boiling salted water for 5 to 7 minutes, or until just tender. (They should still be crisp.) Rinse them under cold running water and drain them well. Place the beans in a salad bowl. Cut the mushroom caps and stems in julienne strips and add them to the beans with the walnuts and salt and pepper to taste. Add the lemon juice and oil and toss. Let mixture marinate at room temperature for 1 hour.

Note: *Select beans carefully. The smaller and greener the better, as they are to be used whole. Also, walnut oil contributes a rich and nutty flavor to this recipe. It is available at gourmet and food stores and better markets.*

OREO ICE CREAM

Serves 4–6

1 quart vanilla ice cream, softened
2½ cups crumbled vanilla-cream-filled
chocolate wafer cookies (Oreos)

In a large bowl combine the softened ice cream and the cookies. Pour the mixture into a serving dish, cover and refreeze.

Christmas Ham Dinner

Christmas Eve has a special quality all its own. It is a quiet time during the busy holiday season when families gather together to attend church services or just to spend the evening in each other's company. From the tiny, mouth-watering biscuits to the rich and tasty plum pudding, this traditional Southern menu is the perfect accompaniment for such an evening and serves up to 12 people. Although this menu has many elements of a traditional Christmas Eve dinner, there are surprises as well: the crabmeat appetizer, the delicate minted peas and onion rice, and finally the flans—a Southern delicacy and an unusual alternative to baked or candied sweet potatoes. Because the ham is best served luke-warm, you can plan to take it out of the oven up to an hour before the meal and utilize that time to prepare other dishes.

Hot Crabmeat Canapés
Salad of Persimmon, Grapefruit, and Endive
Smithfield Ham   Sweet-Potato Flans
Bitty Buttermilk Biscuits
Wild Rice with Minted Peas and Pearl Onions
Plum Pudding with Hard Sauce

HOT CRABMEAT CANAPÉS
Serves 12

1 7-ounce package cream cheese, softened
4 ounces (1 stick) butter, softened
1 7-ounce can crabmeat
1 teaspoon Worcestershire sauce
½ small onion, chopped

In a food processor, blend cream cheese with the butter. Add remaining ingredients and process. Spread on slices of pumpernickel bread and broil until bubbly and brown.

SALAD OF PERSIMMON, GRAPEFRUIT, AND ENDIVE
Serves 12

4 endives
4 persimmons, cut in thin wedges
3 large grapefruit, peeled and sectioned
1 pomegranate

Arrange 4 to 6 endive leaves on each plate in a fan shape. Place a wedge of persimmon between each endive leaf. Divide grapefruit sections equally among the plates, placing them at the base of the fan. Spoon the dressing of your choice over each plate. Sprinkle with pomegranate seeds.

SMITHFIELD HAM
Serves 15 to 20

1 whole sugar-cured ham, uncooked
Water
1 cup brown sugar
2 tablespoons prepared hot mustard
Whole cloves

Scrub ham well. Soak overnight, changing water once. Drain. Cover with fresh water and simmer 15 to 20 minutes per pound. Cool ham in water. Drain; remove skin and all but a thin layer of fat. Cool completely. Slash fat in a diamond pattern. Mix brown sugar and mustard and spread over ham. Press a whole clove into each diamond. Bake ham at 325° for 45 minutes. Cool to lukewarm and slice *very* thin.

SWEET-POTATO FLANS
Serves 12

1 cup sweet-potato puree
¼ teaspoon ground ginger
4 eggs, well beaten
2 tablespoons butter, melted
½ cup heavy cream
⅔ cup milk
Salt and pepper
*2 pounds fresh spinach, washed and
    stemmed*
6 tablespoons melted butter

Preheat oven to 375°.

Generously butter and flour 12 dariole or small soufflé molds. Beat puree, ginger, and eggs together well. Beat in butter, cream, milk, and salt and pepper to taste. Fill each mold about ¾ full. Set molds in a pan of boiling water and bake for 30 minutes. Allow to cool in the molds for about 15 minutes.

Meanwhile, cook spinach in water and drain well. Season with salt and pepper and toss in melted butter. Arrange on a serving platter and unmold flans onto spinach.

BITTY BUTTERMILK BISCUITS

Makes about 2 dozen

2 cups flour
2½ teaspoons baking powder
½ teaspoon baking soda
3 tablespoons butter, chilled
1 cup buttermilk
⅛ teaspoon salt
1 tablespoon sugar (optional)

Sift the flour, baking powder, and baking soda into the bowl of a food processor. Cut the butter into small pieces and add to the flour. Process until it resembles coarse meal. Add the buttermilk, salt, and optional sugar and process until blended. Cover dough and refrigerate for 30 minutes.

Preheat oven to 375°.

Turn dough out on a lightly floured board and pat to a ½-inch thickness. Cut into rounds the size of a half dollar. Bake on an ungreased cookie sheet 15 minutes or until lightly browned. Biscuits may also be dropped by tablespoonfuls onto an ungreased cookie sheet.

WILD RICE WITH MINTED PEAS AND PEARL ONIONS

Serves 12

3 cups Wild Rice (see "Cook's Miscellany" section)
1 pound peas (fresh or frozen)
5 tablespoons butter
½ pound pearl onions, peeled
1 tablespoon chopped fresh mint
1 teaspoon sugar
Salt and pepper

Cook the rice and set aside. Steam the peas over boiling water until tender. Remove from heat. Melt the butter in a saucepan and add the peas, onion, mint, and sugar. Toss and cook for 2 minutes over medium heat. Season with salt and pepper. Gently toss with the wild rice.

PLUM PUDDING WITH HARD SAUCE

Serves 10–12

1 pound seeded raisins
1 pound currants
½ pound citron, chopped
1 cup flour
½ pound butter, softened
½ teaspoon salt
1 cup brown sugar
6 eggs, well beaten
2 cups bread crumbs
1 cup milk
1 whole nutmeg, grated
4 tablespoons brandy
  Sherry to taste
  Hard Sauce (recipe follows)

Dredge the fruits in all but 2 tablespoons of the flour. In a separate bowl, cream together the butter, salt, and sugar. Blend in the eggs. Scald the bread crumbs in the milk. Add to the batter with remaining flour. Add the nutmeg, brandy, and sherry, and blend well. Pour batter into well-greased coffee tins or decorative molds. Cover with waxed paper and secure tightly with string. Place on a rack in a large kettle. Add enough water to come halfway up the sides. Cover kettle and steam pudding for 6 hours, replenishing boiling water as necessary. Store in a cool place or in the refrigerator. Steam for 2 hours before serving. Serve with Hard Sauce.

Note: *Plum pudding may be made from several weeks up to one year in advance and allowed to ripen.*

HARD SAUCE

Makes 1½ cups

8 ounces unsalted butter, softened
1½ cups confectioners' sugar
5 tablespoons brandy
  Pinch of nutmeg (optional)

In the bowl of a food processor, blend together the butter and sugar. Add the brandy and optional nutmeg. Process until smooth and creamy. Put in a tightly covered jar and refrigerate. Serve at room temperature.

Costume Party for
Young Teenagers

Fourteen-year-olds would like you to think that nothing pleases them, but don't believe it for a minute. Offer them a chance to spend an afternoon or evening with their friends and give them an ice-breaking party theme to latch on to, and that familiar oh-so-cool attitude will evaporate like magic.

No matter what theme you choose, the food featured here will appeal to young people of all ages. Vary and substitute freely, but don't even think of serving such adult delicacies as pâté or smoked trout. We invented the ice-cream "volcano" because most young teens are fascinated by anything that has drama and unpredictability. But you, or your caterer, can create an ice-cream sculpture in whatever shape you think will capture their imagination.

Pink Punch   Assorted Soft Drinks

Cheesy Ham Dip   Tortilla Chips and Assorted Crackers

Teenieburgers   Make-Your-Own Heroes

Pizza Muffins

Tomato Kabobs   Hands-On Vegetables

Strawberry Volcano

PINK PUNCH

Makes about 4 gallons

6 cans (6 ounces each) frozen pink-lemon-
 ade concentrate, partly thawed
6 packages frozen sliced strawberries, partly
 thawed
6 cans (6 ounces each) frozen orange-juice
 concentrate
8 quarts ginger ale
4 quarts soda water
 Ice

In each of two large punch bowls, combine halved amounts of all ingredients.
 Stir until frozen lemonade and strawberries soften and break up. Add ice and serve.

CHEESY HAM DIP

Makes about 3 cups

3 cans (4½ ounces each) deviled ham
¼ cup minced onion
3 tablespoons yellow mustard
9 ounces cream cheese, softened
⅓ cup milk
½ cup diced processed cheese

Blend all ingredients except processed
cheese. Add more milk if dip is too stiff. Fold
in diced cheese.

TEENIEBURGERS

Makes about 24 burgers

12 hamburger rolls
 3 pounds ground beef, not too lean
 Salt
 Chili sauce
 Catsup
 Grated onion
 Shredded lettuce

Open the hamburger rolls and use a 2-
inch cookie cutter to cut them into small
rounds. Discard scraps or reserve for another
use. Store cutouts in plastic bag. Shape ground
beef into small, thick patties (about ⅛ pound
each). Heat a heavy skillet and sprinkle with
salt. Cook patties to desired doneness. Serve
burgers in roll cutouts, surrounded by bowls
of chili sauce, catsup, onion, and lettuce.

MAKE-YOUR-OWN HEROS

Serves 12

12 small hero rolls
 2 pounds sliced salami
 1 pound sliced Swiss cheese
 1 pound sliced American cheese
 2 pounds bologna or ham
 4 tomatoes, sliced
 2 cups Mayonnaise (see "Cook's Miscellany" section)
 1 cup yellow mustard
 6 half-sour dill pickles, sliced
 2 cups chopped green peppers

Split rolls and arrange on platter or in serving basket. Arrange meats, cheeses, and tomatoes on a large serving dish. Set condiments out in small bowls. Invite guests to help themselves.

PIZZA MUFFINS
Serves 12

12 English muffins
5 cups bottled or canned pizza sauce
  Oregano
4 cups grated Parmesan cheese
6 cups grated mozzarella cheese
½ pound pepperoni, thinly sliced

Preheat broiler. Split English muffins and spread each half with pizza sauce. Sprinkle with oregano and Parmesan cheese. Shake a generous amount of mozzarella on each. Lay several slices of pepperoni on top of each muffin half. Broil until cheese is melted and edges of pepperoni are slightly curled.

TOMATO KABOBS
Serves 12

12 medium onions
12 strips bacon, halved crosswise
12 large tomatoes

Peel the onions and plunge them into boiling water. Cook for 3 minutes; submerge in cold water. Drain well and cut lengthwise into thick slices.

Cook the bacon until it is almost done but not yet crisp. Fold each strip loosely in half.

Core the tomatoes and cut into fat wedges.

Preheat broiler. Thread tomatoes, onion slices, and folded bacon on metal skewers and broil until bacon is crisp and tomatoes are bubbly.

HANDS-ON VEGETABLES
Serves 12

60 cherry tomatoes
2 cups prepared cream cheese and chive
  dip
  Milk
1 bunch carrots, trimmed, peeled, and cut
  into sticks
4 bunches scallions, trimmed
6 green peppers, cored and sliced in rings

Trim cherry tomatoes and squeeze out the seeds. Thin cream-cheese dip with milk until it has the consistency of pudding. Fill each cherry tomato with about 1 tablespoon of dip. Arrange cherry tomatoes, carrot sticks, scallions, and green pepper rings on serving platter. Spoon remaining chive dip into small bowl and place into center of vegetable platter.

STRAWBERRY VOLCANO

Serves 12

1½ gallons vanilla ice cream, slightly
    softened
6 packages frozen strawberries or
    raspberries
Sugar

Chill a large, deep mixing bowl or wok. Rinse it with very cold water but do not dry. Pack the ice cream into the bowl and place in the freezer until very firm.

Thaw the berries and run them through a blender. Sweeten the puree, if necessary, and refrigerate.

At serving time, unmold the ice cream on a large platter or pizza pan. Scoop about 1 cup out of the top of the mold and pour the strawberry or raspberry puree into the "crater" until much of the "lava" runs down the sides of the volcano.

Picnic in the Park

Bring additional romance to an already memorable setting such as an outdoor concert with a sophisticated picnic. Enhance the picturesque setting by bringing a pretty covering for the ground such as a pastel quilt, a basket of garden flowers, a decorative ice bucket, and pretty stemware for sipping a chilled white wine while savoring the evening. This menu was composed as much for color as for its unusual combination of tastes. Don't be disarmed by the thought of seven types of onions in a pasta dish. The finished effect is subtle and pleasurable.

Sliced Chicken Breast with Basil Mayonnaise
Vegetable Salad with Chive-Mustard Vinaigrette
Green and White Tortellini with Seven Onions
Whole Wheat French Bread   Butter in Pottery Crocks
Fresh Fruit and Cheese   Chilled White Wine

SLICED CHICKEN BREAST WITH BASIL MAYONNAISE

BASIL MAYONNAISE

1 egg
2 yolks
1 tablespoon white-wine vinegar
1 tablespoon Dijon mustard
Leaves from ½ bunch fresh basil
½ cup olive oil
1½ cups peanut oil

Blend egg, yolks, vinegar, mustard, and basil in a food processor. Slowly add oils while blending. Season to taste.

CHICKEN

Serves 4

4 chicken breasts, boned and halved,
  skin on
Salt and pepper
Fresh basil
8 lemon slices

Preheat oven to 400°.
Loosen skin and season chicken under skin with salt, pepper, and fresh basil. Slip lemon slices between skin and meat. Roast for 25 to 30 minutes. Cool and slice thinly across the breast. Serve with a dollop of Basil Mayonnaise.

VEGETABLE SALAD WITH CHIVE-MUSTARD VINAIGRETTE

Serves 4

SALAD

½ pound string beans, trimmed
1 small head broccoli, cut in florets
1 small head cauliflower, cut in florets
3 tomatoes, cut in wedges
1 large zucchini, sliced
5 carrots, cut in sticks
1 red pepper, cut in strips
1 yellow pepper, cut in strips
Watercress
Lemon wedges

Steam string beans, broccoli, and cauliflower until crisply tender. Chill. Arrange with other vegetables on platter and serve with Chive-Mustard Vinaigrette.

CHIVE-MUSTARD VINAIGRETTE

¼ cup Dijon mustard
½ cup red-wine vinegar
¾ cup olive oil
¾ cup peanut oil
½ cup snipped chives
Tabasco
Salt and freshly ground white pepper

In a bowl, whisk together mustard and vinegar; then slowly whisk in oils. Season to taste with Tabasco, salt, and pepper.

GREEN AND WHITE TORTELLINI WITH SEVEN ONIONS

 3 tablespoons olive oil
¼ cup chopped leeks
½ cup thinly sliced shallots
¼ cup chopped Spanish onions
¼ cup chopped red onions
¼ cup sliced pearl onions
⅛ cup minced garlic
¼ cup sliced scallions
¼ cup snipped chives
 2 cups green tortellini
2 cups white tortellini
 Salt and pepper
 Red-wine vinegar
 Fresh parsley
 Fresh basil

Heat 2 tablespoons olive oil and sauté first five onions and garlic. Let cool; then add scallions and chives.

Cook the tortellini in boiling, salted water with remaining 1 tablespoon olive oil until *al dente*. Drain and refresh in cold water. Toss with onion mixture. Season with salt, pepper, vinegar, parsley, and basil.

The Cocktail Party

That ubiquitous American institution the Cocktail Party can be as lavish as a banquet or as simple as a bowl of peanuts. Its size depends on the occasion; its menu possibilities are limitless.

Following the menu card below are some guidelines to help you plan the cocktail party of your liking.

Tiropetes
Scotch Eggs
Hot Crab Dip
Spicy Clam Pie
Stuffed Mushrooms
Cheese Beignets with Monterey Jack and Cilantro
Jicama Rounds with Smoked Turkey and Red-Pepper Mousse

SOME SUGGESTIONS

- People like to know what they are eating, in particular those with food allergies. Limit yourself to no more than 7 types of hors-d'oeuvres—but make them smashing. Offer a wide variety, including some crunchy, some smooth, some bland, some sharp. Serve old stand-bys as well as innovative recipes.
- Think through the presentation of the hors-d'oeuvres. How will they look after they're exposed to the air awhile? Best to arrange them in small serving dishes, replenishing them frequently, so that they always look appetizing. Garnishing the serving dishes is important: flowers, sprigs of parsley, lemon and tomato roses, and the like are all attractive choices.
- Restrict each tray to one or two types of hors-d'oeuvre. You don't want conversations interrupted unnecessarily as guests ponder what morsel to select.
- Don't make your guests work for what they eat. Rule out anything that they would have to slice or spread themselves—or, if you are set on serving hors-d'oeuvres of this sort, slice and spread ahead of time. For example, cut cheese or apply cheese spread to crackers before offering them to your guests.
- Avoid runny dips. They drip.
- Steer clear of foods requiring cocktail plates. They are awkward for guests to handle and they crowd up valuable table space.
- Give canapés a professional look by topping them with slivers of nuts, radishes, scallion, green or red pepper, celery, olive, crumbled bacon, egg yolk, touches of dill, parsley, tarragon, or mint.
- To keep bread or canapés fresh, spread them with a layer of butter before adding the filling. Arrange on serving trays and insert toothpicks to hold the plastic wrapping away from the canapés. Cover with plastic wrap or foil. Chill until serving time.
- Buffet tables demand constant attention. They will start looking sloppy if someone isn't in frequent attendance to replenish trays, pick up abandoned glasses, and empty ashtrays. Don't make one table the sole location for hors-d'oeuvres. Most guests will be too busy talking to make a special trip to a central location.
- When preparing canapés for a crowd, speed up the process by setting up a conveyer-belt system. Do all of the buttering, then all of the filling. Spread the work out on a dining-room table if your kitchen counter space is limited.
- To figure the amount of liquor you will need, consult your liquor store about how much to order. Since unopened bottles are returnable, it's better to overorder. Drinking tastes vary enormously around the country, although there is a distinct trend toward lighter drinking, and particularly toward wine. Don't get jugs of wine for a crowd; they are large and difficult to handle. Two or three small bottles, chilled if appropriate and replenished according to need, is a more tasteful and practical alternative.
- Allow one glass per guest per hour. The trend is to serve all drinks in stemmed glassware rather than in tumbler-type glasses. Stemware is easier to handle, doesn't sweat or drip as much, and is more elegant-looking.
- For drinks before dinner, a safe rule of thumb is to allow a tray of ice per person and to make it ahead of time, saving it in plastic bags. This amount may vary according to the temperature, the length of the party, and what people are drinking. Champagne and wine parties require a lot of ice for chilling the bottles (a case of wine, which will yield 75 glasses, requires 20 pounds of ice).
- To arrive at the amount of mixers and soft drinks you'll need, figure on one bottle per person and divide the result equally between club soda, tonic, ginger ale, cola, and diet drinks.

TIROPETES

Makes 2½ dozen

3 ounces cream cheese, softened
5 ounces Feta cheese, crumbled
3 ounces Gruyère, shredded
1 egg, beaten
2 tablespoons chopped parsley
10 sheets phyllo dough, thawed in
    refrigerator
Melted butter
Egg wash

Preheat oven to 375°.

Mix together cheeses, egg, and parsley. Remove pastry from box and cover with a damp cloth to keep it from drying out. Working rapidly, take out one sheet of pastry and cover others. Paint phyllo sheet with butter. Using a very sharp knife, cut pastry lengthwise into 3 strips. Place a tablespoon of cheese filling in the bottom-right-hand corner of each strip. Fold over pastry as you would fold a flag. Place triangular packets on a baking sheet and paint with egg wash. Bake for 10 minutes until golden brown. Serve hot.

Note: *Tiropetes may be cooled and then frozen. To reheat, place frozen pastries on a baking sheet and heat at 375° for 10 minutes.*

SCOTCH EGGS

Serves 24

12 medium eggs, hard-boiled
1 pound bulk sausage
2 eggs, beaten
1 bottle beer or ale
    Seasoned bread crumbs

Preheat oven to 350°.

Peel eggs. Flatten sausage on waxed paper. With wet hands, peel up a thin layer of sausage and wrap around each hard-boiled egg. When completely covered with sausage, dip in beaten egg and then in beer or ale. Roll in bread crumbs. Place eggs on a rack in a roasting pan and bake for 45 to 60 minutes or until sausage is browned. Serve at room temperature with a robust, grainy mustard.

Note: *These may be made one day in advance and stored in the refrigerator. Re-crisp in oven before serving.*

HOT CRAB DIP

Serves 24

19 ounces cream cheese
1 large can crabmeat, drained
¼–½ cup milk
½ cup Mayonnaise (see "Cook's Miscellany" section)
½ teaspoon garlic powder

1/4 teaspoon lemon juice
1/4 teaspoon Worcestershire sauce
2 teaspoons minced onion
2 drops Tabasco

Melt cream cheese in a double boiler over medium heat. Stir in remaining ingredients until well blended. Refrigerate one day to blend flavors. Reheat in double boiler or chafing dish and serve on rounds of French bread.

SPICY CLAM PIE

Serves 20

4 7 1/2-ounce cans chopped clams
4 teaspoons lemon juice
2 onions, finely chopped
2 green peppers, finely chopped
1/2 cup chopped parsley
3/4 cup clam juice
2 sticks butter
2 tablespoons oregano
4 teaspoons Tabasco
1/2 teaspoon pepper
1 1/2 cups grated mozzarella
Paprika

Preheat oven to 325°.
Drain clams and reserve 3/4 to 1 cup of their juice. Simmer clams and lemon juice over low heat for 1 minute. Stir in onions, peppers, parsley, and enough clam juice to moisten. Add butter and seasonings. Cook over low heat until butter melts. Stir in bread crumbs. Spoon mixture into two shallow pie plates or casserole dishes. Sprinkle with mozzarella and bake for 25 minutes. Remove from oven and sprinkle with paprika. Serve hot with melba toast or sturdy crackers.

STUFFED MUSHROOMS

1 1/2 pounds white mushrooms, medium-large size
3 tablespoons butter

Wipe mushrooms clean and remove stems. Chop stems and add to filling. Brush mushrooms with butter and place in a roasting pan. Fill hollows with desired filling, top with grated cheese, and bake in a preheated 375° oven for 15 minutes or until caps are tender.

FILLINGS
Sauté shallots with mushroom stems and mix in bread crumbs, chopped parsley, grated Swiss, and grated Parmesan.
Sauté onions and stems mixed with bread crumbs, crabmeat, chopped parsley, and a dash of Worcestershire sauce.
Sauté onions and mushroom stems with chopped ham and grated Swiss cheese.

CHEESE BEIGNETS WITH MONTEREY JACK AND CILANTRO

Makes about 24 beignets

$2/3$ cup water
$1/2$ stick butter
$2^1/2$ ounces sifted all-purpose flour
2 large eggs
2 ounces Monterey Jack cheese, grated
2 tablespoons cilantro, finely chopped, or
    $1^1/2$ teaspoons dried cilantro
3 drops Tabasco
$1/2$ teaspoon salt
    Dash of cayenne pepper
    Oil for deep-frying
    Sauce Rémoulade (recipe follows)

In a heavy saucepan bring water and butter to a boil. Add sifted flour, stirring vigorously with a wire whisk or wooden spoon to incorporate fully. Off the heat, continue to beat the mixture with an electric mixer, adding the eggs, cheese, cilantro, and other seasonings. Beat until fully incorporated. Set aside until ready to fry.

Into a heavy-bottomed saucepan pour enough vegetable oil to reach 1 inch up the sides of the pan. Over a moderate flame, heat the oil to 375°. While the oil is heating, use a teaspoon to form small balls with the diameter of a quarter. (If the mixture becomes too sticky to work with, coat your hands with flour and roll balls into uniform sizes.) When the oil reaches 375°, drop the balls into the pan and fry until golden brown, about 8 minutes, and drain on paper towels. Serve hot with Sauce Rémoulade.

SAUCE RÉMOULADE

Makes $1^1/2$ cups

2 egg yolks
$1^1/4$ cups vegetable oil
$1/2$ cup celery, finely chopped
$1/2$ cup scallions, finely chopped
$1/4$ cup fresh parsley
$1/4$ cup prepared horseradish
    Grated skin and juice of 1 lemon
2 tablespoons hot mustard
2 tablespoons ketchup
2 tablespoons Worcestershire sauce
1 tablespoon red or white wine vinegar
1 tablespoon Tabasco

1 tablespoon minced garlic
2 teaspoons Hungarian paprika
2 teaspoons white pepper
1 teaspoon salt

In a blender or food processor, process the egg yolks for 2 minutes. With the machine running, add the oil in a thin stream. One at a time, blend in the remaining ingredients until well mixed. Chill well.

JICAMA ROUNDS WITH SMOKED TURKEY AND RED-PEPPER MOUSSE

Makes 24 rounds

1 teapoon unsalted butter
4 fleshy red peppers, cored, seeded, and cut
    into 1/4-inch strips
1 medium clove garlic, minced
    Pinch of dried thyme
1 tablespoon white-wine vinegar
1 teaspoon unflavored gelatin
3/4 cup heavy cream, chilled
    Salt to taste
1/4 teaspoon white pepper
1 jicama, peeled
6 slices smoked turkey breast, thinly sliced
    and cut into 1 1/4-inch rounds
    Cilantro or watercress leaves

Melt butter in a saucepan and add peppers, garlic, and thyme. Cook, stirring occasionally to prevent burning, about 15–20 minutes. Transfer the mixture to a food processor and puree until smooth. Press mixture through a sieve to remove pepper skins. Discard skins and reserve puree. Soften the gelatin in the vinegar. Combine with puree in a small saucepan and heat without boiling. Stir to dissolve gelatin completely. Remove from heat and cool over ice. Beat heavy cream to soft peaks and fold into pepper puree, mixing thoroughly. Season with salt and pepper. Chill until ready to assemble hors-d'oeuvres.

Cut jicama into 1/4-inch-thick slices and then into 1 1/2-inch rounds. Keep in icewater until ready to assemble. Drain jicama on paper towel. Top each round with a round of smoked turkey breast. Using a pastry bag with a star tip, pipe an appropriate amount of mousse onto the smoked turkey. Garnish with a sprig of cilantro or watercress.

PART FOUR

Flowers, Flowers, Flowers

Working with Flowers

Florist's Tools

Working with flowers is not unlike cooking: Both require a few tools, a sink, and decent counter space. Both also create a mess in order to achieve the desired results. To make the cleanup easy, a sheet of plastic on the floor and over the workspace will come in handy. The basic tools you will need include the following:

Cutting equipment

A small, sharp knife, ideally a jack knife with a dull point at the end, although a short kitchen knife will do. This is indispensable for cutting stems on the diagonal. Never use scissors: They tend to bruise delicate flower stems. You'll need the knife also for trimming excess foliage, cutting away knobs or shoots, stripping tough stems.

Florist's scissors, or stub scissors, with serrated cutting edges, tough enough to cut thicker branches and wire.

Secateurs, or pruning shears, for heavy foliage.

Scissors, the everyday variety, for cutting tape and string and trimming brown, ragged edges of leaves.

Other equipment

Hammer to smash the ends of woody stems for better water absorption.

Pails. Tall and short plastic ones with collapsible lifting handles. Filled with a few inches of water for gathering flowers from the garden or woods and for storing flowers in deep water before conditioning.

Plastic watering can, one with a long, narrow spout for adding water to flower-filled vases.

Plastic spray bottle filled with water to mist arrangements daily.

Plastic liners to waterproof straw or vine baskets and other porous or rust-prone receptacles. Leftover food container of all sizes and shapes as well as sandwich and small garbage bags come in handy

Items for holding flowers

Pin holders or needle holders, also known as "frogs." These round or rectangular metal-weighted devices, looking like miniature beds of nails, are used to secure stems into position when arranging flowers. Particularly suited to shallow containers or for stylized arrangements where very little plant material is to be used.

Plastic foam. Dense bricks or cylinders of a water-retentive green sponge into which flower stems are pushed for support. Known also as "floral foam," "green foam," and "Oasis." Must be soaked in water for two hours before using and can be cut, dry or wet, to fit almost any container. Once "waterlogged," the foam must remain wet if it is to be used again. To prevent drying out, store in an airtight plastic bag with a little bit of extra water.

Foam should be cut to extend an inch or more above the rim of the container so that stems and foliage can be inserted from the sides. It should also be shaped to leave enough space at the sides to add additional water daily.

Chicken wire or wire netting. Mesh with one-inch holes is the most practical size. To figure approximately how much wire you need for the size of the container, measure a piece that is as wide as the flower holder and three times its depth. Crumple the wire into a loose free-form that conforms to the shape of the container; it should extend above the edges so that flowers can be inserted at both vertical and horizontal angles. Chicken wire is often used as additional support placed over pin holders or green foam.

Sand or gravel. A quick and inexpensive medium to anchor flowers with tough stems. Fill a deep vase to two thirds with stone and top with water. Also used to raise the level of a pin holder or foam with deep or tall containers.

Clear glass vases are often enhanced with the addition of shells, marbles, or polished stones. They also provide ballast for top-heavy flowers.

Floral waterproof tape, used to anchor foam, pin holders or wire netting to a container. Readily camouflaged with foliage.

Floral wire. Eighteen-gauge green, plastic-laminated wire is useful for reinforcing fragile flower heads and stems.

Containers

Today, anything goes in the choice of a container for the flowers you want to display. Time was when you were limited to conventional "vahzes" or "vayses," receptacles reserved exclusively for holding water and flower stems. (One was a wedding present; the other the remains of an arrangement delivered by the florist.) Contemporary flower arranging encourages the imaginative use of any number of improvised items about the house—from straw baskets to silver tea caddies. Passé, however, is anything that goes overboard on the side of fussiness or coyness. Simplicity of design and proportion is your best guideline. Keep your eyes open for holders about the house that lend themselves to moonlighting. Without doubt the most harmonious arrangement of all is a bouquet of flowers standing artlessly in a simple pitcher. Unless you are a hobbyist, it's a waste of valuable space to store shelves of bulky, seldom-used dust collectors.

The most versatile shapes for arrangements are tall, narrow cylinders, round bowls, and shallow oblongs. Your selection will be based not only on the height, shape, and color of the container in relation to the flowers but on where you want to put the arrangement, and on the occasion itself. Clearly the requirements for a composition intended for a long buffet table will be dramatically different from one designed for a bedroom side table. And what is appropriate in a country setting might look out of place in a formal or modern drawing room.

Since there *are* no hard-and-fast rules about containers, rely on your eye. As long as the container enhances rather than overwhelms the flowers, it serves its purpose well. Incidentally, for those occasions when you need to rely on a florist for a party arrangement, take appropriate containers with you to the shop and discuss your needs.

Some Foliages, Backgrounds and Fillers for Arrangements

Airy	
Fern Asparagus (Plumosus) Dagger Jade Maidenhair Ming Rock Sprengeri Tree (Tiki)	**Vine** Grape Honeysuckle Ivy (English, Needlepoint, Variegated) Smilax
Grass Cattail Cloud Bamboo Bullgrass Elephant Quaking Timothy	**Other** Aralia Baby's breath Corkscrew (Curly) willow Dill Euphorbia Forsythia Queen Anne's lace Scotch broom

Dense		
Aspidistra	Galax	Magnolia
Boxwood	Holly	Myrtle
Camellia	Hosta	Palm
Croton	Huckleberry	Pittosporum
Draecena	Kale (ornamental)	Podocarpus
Dusty miller	Laurel	Rhododendron
Eucalyptus	Leatherleaf	Ruscus
Euonymus	Lemon leaves	Ti leaves

FLOWERING HOUSE PLANTS—SUITABLE FOR TABLE ARRANGEMENTS

Type	Colors
African Violet	*lavender, purple, blue, white*
Ageratum	*blue, white*
Azalea	*pink, red, salmon, white*
Begonia	*red, white, pink, salmon*
Cactus	*varied*
Christmas Cactus	*pink, red, salmon, white*
Chrysanthemum	*varied*
Crocus	*varied*
Daffodil	*yellow, white*
Dianthus	*varied*
Geranium	*red, white, pink, salmon*
Gerbera Daisy	*varied*
Hydrangea	*pink, white, blue, green*
Impatiens	*red, white, pink, salmon*
Lily	*varied*
Marigold	*yellow, orange*
Orchids	*varied*
Petunia	*varied*
Poinsettia	*red, white, pink*
Tulip	*varied*
Zinnia	*varied*

Selection, Preparation, and Care of Flowers

You can't go wrong with fresh water and a container when arranging flowers and foliage in your home. But why not prolong for as long as possible the pleasure and luxury of beautiful flowers? By following a few fundamental steps in preparing them for display, you can considerably enhance and prolong the vase-life of your flowers.

Selection

People living in cities and towns have to rely on florists, outdoor stands, and even supermarkets for their plant life. They are not to be pitied. Most commercially grown flowers have been raised under the best of conditions. And today, the variety available year round is greater than ever with the astounding proliferation of imported flowers from Holland, Israel, South America, and other agricultural areas. Many factors revolving around the shipping-and-handling process affect the future vase-life of the flowers you purchase, but if you look for those in peak condition, odds are that you will be satisfied. A good guide to ensure longevity is to check for well-formed buds and for flowers with pale centers. Reject those that have developed to the seed stage or that have leaves or stems that look tired.

In the long run, it pays dividends to search out a reliable florist and establish a good rapport with him. It may be slightly more expensive, but a quality florist shop won't sell you flowers that have been refrigerated too long or damaged through improper care. A caring florist can be counted on as well for counsel in arranging flowers for important occasions—not to mention the tips you will learn through your shared interest.

Flowers from the garden or the wilds should be picked in early morning or in the evening, when their stems are at their strongest. At midday they have lost most of their moisture to the heat of the sun, and you may have trouble reviving them. *How* you pick flowers is important. Carry a sharp knife and a bucket partially filled with tepid water. Since a plant is 90 percent water, every moment it is deprived of moisture is a threat to its survival. Cut at an angle to expose more capillary surface to water. (Do not pinch, break, tear, or cut with scissors, as that squeezes off the stem's ability to draw moisture.) Try to cut stems just *above* the leaf node; this encourages new growth for the remaining plant. Later, at home, cutting *below* the plant nodes assures the flower of vital nutrients. If the stems are tough or woody, slit them crosswise about one inch up from the bottom of the stem and scrape off any bark at the base. Many people assume that a draft of cold water would be refreshing to a thirsty plant, but cold water may ac-

tually throw delicate flowers into shock. The closer the water is to outdoor temperature, the better the stems will take to it.

Soaking

As soon as you get the flowers home, fill the water bucket up to neck level and let the plants rest for a while in a shady, cool spot until you proceed to prepare them further.

Conditioning

Conditioning is the process that can add days to the life of cut plant materials. The techniques vary, and in fact are the subject of endless debate and experiment among florists, horticulturists, and experienced flower arrangers. But the basics are pretty much the same, all of them designed to ensure a steady supply of water circulating from the bottom of the stem to the top of the flower head. It's a process also known as "hardening," for if the flowers are filled with water to capacity, their stems will remain turgid and their heads erect.

While the experts may not agree on methods, they do concur that bacteria growth in the water is the outstanding threat to the health and longevity of cut flowers. Bacteria are what cut off and clog the vital supply of water that is life for a plant. It is for this reason that plant hygiene is so important. Keep all equipment scrub-clean. Wash buckets, containers, wire netting, pin holders, and all other tools with a mild disinfectant after each use. Another villain is decay from leaves left underwater to rot. They create matter that not only clogs the stems but makes the water cloudy and smelly (a few drops of household bleach in vase water is a help). Strip all foliage from that part of the flower stems that will rest below the water level, as well as much that will appear above. The idea is to make a direct path for the water being drawn up through the stem to the flower head.

Another step before treating flowers to the conditioning bath is to recut the stems, as it is important to remove any sticky seal or air bubbles that may have formed while exposed, however briefly, to the elements. Cut at a slant to the approximate length you will want in your final arrangement, but do this with the flower stems submerged in water (a kitchen sink is fine) to prevent any air pockets.

Some flowers respond to a little extra attention before conditioning. Though techniques outlined below are not crucial for their survival, certain species will respond to them with alacrity. Consult the flower chart that follows for the specific flowers that will benefit from special treatment.

Fibrous, woody, and hard stems. Plants and flowering shrubs and trees with thick or hard-surfaced stems need help to expose more cells to water than an angled cut can provide. Open up their inner tissues for more rapid water absorption by crushing the stem ends lightly with a hammer, or by making two one- to two-inch upward slits in the stems with a sharp knife. Plants with a thick bark benefit additionally if you scrape or peel off this waterproof layering at the base of the stem before crushing or splitting.

Hollow stems. Delphinium, amaryllis, and other hollow-stemmed flowers last longer if the stems are filled with cold water and then plugged with cotton. Hold the stems upside down and fill them under the tap or with the aid of a small funnel placed in the stem end.

Milky stems. Some flower stems "bleed" a sticky latex sap when cut. It flows out, and as it dries, it hardens, sealing up the water-conducting cells of the stem ends. This can be treated in one of two ways: 1) applying a flame to the stem ends to the count of a slow 15, or until they are black and no longer sizzling; 2) dipping the ends in boiling water for 30 seconds.

The first method is easier and recommended if there are only a few flowers to treat. The second method is faster and more efficient if you have a quantity of flowers to do. If you choose the latter technique, you'll need to protect the flower heads from the steam and heat. A good method is to fashion a collar out of newspaper. Cut a slit through several thicknesses of paper and push the stems in a bunch through the hole, holding the newspaper loosely around the flowers. Examples of flowers whose stems bleed are poinsettia, stephanotis, butterfly weed, euphorbia, poppy, and dandelion.

Stems with white bases. Some bulb flowers such as daffodils, tulips, and hyacinths have stems whose milky-white part will not absorb water. Simply cut the white part off and rinse the stem of any lingering sap under cool running water.

Total immersion. Mature foliage such as ferns, galax, ivy, stems, and vines can absorb water directly through soaking for at least two hours, preferably overnight, without harm. Younger, more delicate foliage is more susceptible to waterlogging and should not be kept immersed for great lengths of time. The one exception: Gray foliage does not take well to complete immersion.

After your flowers have been recut underwater and you have completed any preconditioning treatment, immediately begin soaking the flowers "neck high" in a clean, nonmetallic container overnight or at least for a couple of hours. This is to give them a chance to get as much water as possible into the leaf and stem tissues. Thus hardened, they well be ideally suited for the arrangement process.

Many but not all experts treat conditioning water with an additive whose function is to extend the vase-life of the flowers. A general, all-purpose solution is one that adds both a sugar nutrient to the water and a bacteria retardant. The commerical brands on the market such as Flora-Life are excellent. Equally beneficial is the addition of 1 tablespoon of sugar and ¼ teaspoon of bleach per gallon of water, one to provide energy-producing food, the other to keep the water pure. Some people swear copper coins or aspirin extend the vase-life of flowers. We leave such family recipes up to you.

Caring for finished flower arrangements

The greatest payoff for the time you put into preparing your flowers for display is that you need do nothing except add water to the arrangement daily. If the flowers are casually propped in a container without benefit of mechanics, a complete change of water at room temperature and a washing out of the container will prolong the blooms. So as not to disturb a studied arrangement in green foam, use a watering can with a long, narrow spout for "topping" the sides of the container. Long-lasting flowers such as mums and daisies will benefit from a few drops of household bleach in the water. Liberal spraying with a mister will make up for the lack of humidity in the rooms, but remove the arrangement to the kitchen or bathroom before doing so. A cool place to store the flowers overnight will also help to slow drying out. An alternate trick to retain moisture is to cover the arrangement loosely with a plastic bag, creating a humidity chamber.

Fundamentals of Flower Design

You do not have to be an award-winning member of the Garden Club to create pleasing flower arrangements. True, there is a certain mystique to the elaborate and often fanciful compositions you see in decorating magazines, but they are not as complicated as they look, since good design follows the dictates of nature. Most of the techniques of traditional flower arranging can be learned by attending lectures, demonstrations, and flower shows, by looking at paintings, and by reading some excellent books on the subject. (See Further Reading.) However, this section is for the novice who feels all thumbs about how to go beyond "plunking" some flowers into a container. True, there *are* fundamental rules of flower arranging, but the only rule for the beginner to remember is: Relax. The rest of the rules, once mastered, are for the breaking anyway.

If you have a basic understanding of what makes for a happy arrangement, then you are on your way to countless designs of your own invention. The components of any flower arrangement can be broken down into four elements: shape, color, texture, and harmony. Working together to form a whole, they are the basis of every successful arrangement, no matter how simple or elaborate it may be.

Shape

Most contemporary arrangements fall within a few geometric forms: the circle, the vertical, the horizontal, and, less frequently, the square and the fan. Generally, the shape of your arrangements will evolve spontaneously into one of these forms once you have thought through several factors, such as where you want to place it (in the middle of the dining table, on a sideboard for a buffet, to lend drama to an entrance hall); the shape, size, and height of the flowers you want to use; and the containers you have on hand. By far the most versatile and least demanding of these geometric forms for the novice is the circular or "mass" arrangement.

Color

The first thing that registers when one first sees an arrangement is color. For this reason, it is the element that carries the most emotional impact. You might see excitement in the burst of a brilliant array of colors; tranquillity in a quiet composition of blues and whites; exuberance emanating from an arrangement of spring flowers; urbanity, formality, country rustic, and so on. It is the subtle interplay of colors that produces such reflexive impressions. Your inner color wheel will tell you what colors work well together. You don't need to know that a creative combination of flowers of one color (varying shades of white, for example) is a study in monochrome; that the heather and red tulips in a mirrored container are adjacent colors; or that a holiday-season composition of reds and greens is a complementary arrangement of color opposites.

Texture

Whereas colors are selected for their relationship, textures are mixed for contrast. Glossy and matte, smooth and rough, dense and airy, pearly and prickly, solid and lacy: These tactile qualities give a third, sculptural dimension to flower arrangements.

Technically, visual texture is determined by the degree to which a surface reflects light. Placed side by side, a smooth, glossy flower will upstage a soft, velvety one of the same color. On the other hand, observe how the shiny green leaves of a gardenia flatter the muted white of its blossom.

Subtle interplay of varying shades of white in a monochromatic arrangement.

Juxtaposing textural contrasts in an arrangement is a fascinating exercise in ingenuity. Keep your eye out for unexpected combinations: With a country garden potpourri of garden flowers, add some graceful bare branches for both texture and form. A judicious selection of fruits or vegetables tucked into a mass of flowers adds sculptural interest. Don't overlook the impact of textural contrast between arrangement and container (an antique metal tub holding masses of full-blown garden roses, for example) and between arrangement and setting (bright, glossy flower materials for a dimly lit area; a muted display of fuzzy, velvety ones for a busy background).

Harmony

Obvious as it may seem, don't overlook *how* your arrangement will look in relation to its setting. Shape, color, and texture are crucial to a well-executed composition, but the arrangement itself must be appropriate for both the occasion and the place it is to occupy. For example, a delicate arrangement suitable for a bridal shower might look out of place in an art gallery. And a simple basket of spring flowers is better suited to the bedroom than is an ornate construct belonging on a buffet table.

Before starting your arrangement, picture how the flowers will be viewed by the guests: seated or standing? Consider as well the color scheme and design of the room, as well as the particular table or wall against which it will be seen. You'll want your design to be complementary and harmonious with the design of the room: emphatic colors for light-colored rooms; light, shiny flowers for dark-colored rooms; casual arrangements for informal rooms; dramatically stark compositions for minimalist interiors.

No one can provide a set of rules as to what is proper scale, but if you plan your arrangement *in relation* to the room for which it is intended, the results are bound to be appropriate. Trust your eye: If it's too small, it will look puny, and, no matter how striking the design, if it's too large, it will appear to be overwhelming.

Whether you want a spontaneous or a composed look for your flowers, the success of your arrangement is ensured when you use these elements of shape, color, and texture working harmoniously as an expression of your own personality.

The "mechanics" of a standard arrangement is explained in the section that follows. Once you have experimented with the most basic of arrangements and discover for yourself how much fun it is to work with flowers, you'll be inspired to explore further this fascinating and absorbing avenue of self-expression.

Step-by-Step Techniques of Flower Arranging

Earlier, we explained how the elements of shape, color, texture, and harmony work in unison in the makeup of any floral composition. Now let's take a single arrangement to illustrate how to integrate those components into an elementary design. The most useful—and versatile—one is the traditional round "mass" design commonly used as a centerpiece for the dinner table. It is also the easiest of the basic forms to handle and, once mastered, the springboard for countless other designs. Once again, remember that the steps that follow are general guidelines. The whole point of an arrangement, no matter how much design went into the making, is that it *look* spontaneous and natural and free.

For this basic design, I selected white anemones as the dominant or focal flower, roses for color, and for texture and body I added narcissus, lilac, and dill. When buying or gathering materials for an arrangement, keep in mind the old adage that floral design is never composed of even numbers (three or five daisies in a vase, but never two or four). Don't fret if you find yourself overbuying. Leftover, smaller pieces as accents to the main arrangement give the impression of greater abundance. As soon as the flowers are brought home, treat them to the preparation and soaking process known in the flower trade as "conditioning." (See Selection, Preparation, and Care of Flowers.)

You don't have to limit yourself to traditional vases. For a round container, I chose a standard soufflé dish to illustrate how a simple household utensil can

1. Secure green foam to the container with floral tape. Use floral adhesive to glue galax leaves around the sides of the bowl. Establish the circumference, or frame, of the arrangement with the lead flowers (anemone). Add secondary flowers (roses) to the frame.

2. Introduce your accent and filler flowers (narcissus, lilac).

double effectively as a flower holder. With floral adhesive I stuck a band of galax leaves around the sides of the container, both to make the base a more natural extension of the arrangement and to camouflage the mechanics employed to hold the flowers in position.

To hold the flowers in position, a block of water-soaked green foam is cut to fit the width of the container. The other mechanical aids available are discussed in Florist's Tools, but for the beginner, green foam is the easiest to work with. The foam should not conform precisely to the shape of the container: You need to allow room to extend above the rim of the container so that stems can be inserted at diagonal as well as vertical angles. To stabilize the foam, crisscross floral tape over the foam and onto the rim of the container.

Now the fun begins. Position the first flower at the center of the arrangement. As the tallest flower, or "lead" flower, its height will determine the scale of the entire design. To figure its "right" height, a reliable rule is to trim it to a little more than two times the height or width of the container, whichever is greater.

3. Complete the arrangement by rounding out gaps and spaces where needed, and add an airy element (such as dill) for height and line.

Next, establish the circumference of the circular design at points north, south, east, and west by inserting above the rim of the container four additional stems (slightly shorter than the lead flower) reaching out almost horizontally. These five flowers now form the skeleton of the shape.

Below the apex of the design, form a circle with the secondary flowers (roses) and more anemones. They should be trimmed slightly shorter than the tall flowers.

Add depth and interest to the design by tucking still shorter stems of the secondary flowers inside the outer frame so that they look like inner branches. Near the rim of the container, sink flowers low into the foam so that they appear to spill out over the sides.

Introduce the accent and filler flowers to round out the design with texture and body (narcissus for height, lilac for body, dill for airiness). As you go along it is important to remember to add your materials at different lengths—always at an angle—to give the composition a natural, spontaneous look.

By now you will have discovered the thrill of the arrangement's taking on a life of its own. It will tell *you* where to fill in the gaps and spaces and where to leave well enough alone. All that's left is to reward the flowers with a little extra water and to stand back and admire the live painting you and Mother Nature have created.

Using the same methods described for the round arrangement of white anemones and roses, experiment with other materials to create interesting centerpieces, from casual to elegant, all easy and quick to assemble once you've discovered the magic a little bit of ingenuity will create.

Birthday-party centerpiece. An assortment of brightly striped candy canes turned a soufflé dish into a festive centerpiece literally pretty enough to eat. Surround a bowl with candy sticks, secure with a rubber band, and cover with a pretty gingham ribbon. You might try substituting peppermint canes for a holiday look, sharpened pencils at a bridge party, giant crayons at a children's party—the variations are up to you.

The flowers in this round arrangement combined anemone with iris, dianthus, roses, dusty miller, and baby's breath.

Sunday brunch buffet. Bread, the staff of life, is used as the basis for an unusual "dry" composition combining wheat and pasta as decoration for a fall table. Here the soufflé dish was circled with pasta, held in place with gaily tied ribbon. A variety of dark and light breads form the basis of a mechanics-free still life containing loaves of French bread, round bread, bagels, challah, braided bread, and bread sticks. Strands of corkscrew fussili and natural wheat provide the artistic touch, forcing us to look at the commonplace forms that surround us with renewed respect.

Bar table. Too often at cocktail parties the bar is overlooked as a mere repository for a whole lot of opened bottles. Yet, the bar often becomes the most popular area at a party. Why not dress it up with a festive touch for people to admire while waiting for their drinks? Here lemons and limes in a clear soufflé dish take on an extra dimension with sprigs of mimosa and several pale-green cymbidium. (If the temperature is warm, the flowers will stay fresh longer if protected by water picks.)

Centerpiece for the holidays Once again a soufflé dish demonstrates its versatility in a tall arrangement that would work as well on a sideboard for a cocktail buffet as on a table for a seated dinner.

This arrangement provides an example of a basic rule successfully broken. So as not to block the view of guests talking to each other at the dinner table, centerpieces generally should meet the "elbow on the table to clenched fist" test for appropriate height, and a massed arrangement for the dinner table should not exceed 15 inches high. Tall, airy blossoms and branches such as the ones in this arrangement are increasingly fashionable. As in *all* arrangements, the acid test is to view your arrangements at each stage as you go along—from all sides, standing and seated. Unfortunately, beginners often forget the importance of viewing their arrangements in the context of how they will be viewed in their destined settings. If you assemble your materials while standing, pause frequently to view your progress both

Birthday Party Centerpiece: *Candy canes turn an ordinary soufflé dish into a festive container for a party arrangement.*

Sunday Brunch Buffet: *Create striking centerpieces* without *flowers. Vegetables and fruits are effective; so is a fall arrangement composed solely of pastas and breads.*

206

Bar Table: *For a cocktail party, try dressing up your bar accessories with a floral touch, such as a few cymbidium orchids and sprigs of mimosa and boxwood.*

207

Centerpiece for the Holidays: *A simple but dramatic arrangement composed of red and white branches with bright red miniature amaryllis and gerbera daisies.*

from a standing distance and from up close, and seated if the flowers are to be viewed at the dinner table.

The holiday arrangement pictured here was composed with a winter theme in mind: Bare branches of red and white (readily available at florist shops in December) are locked in position with pin holders or water-soaked green foam. The addition of bright-red miniature amaryllis and giant gerbera daisies above a wreath of boxwood creates a dramatically simple display.

The Language of Flowers

In Queen Victoria's day, people were fascinated by flowers and invested them with sentiments that would have been considered unseemly to express in words. A shy suitor, for example, might send a maiden a bouquet expressing his thoughts about her: buttercup (radiant charm); day lily (coquettish); white hyacinth (quiet loveliness); or purple lilac (first emotions of love). In the same spirit, a young lady might vent her frustration at a ruthless cad by arranging a posy with hydrangea (heartlessness); marigold (jealousy); gladiolus (pain and tears) . . . and tuberose (dangerous pleasure).

Flowers still speak volumes. Though today's vocabulary is more freewheeling, messages of unabashed sentiment are as appropriate as ever. Here are a few thoughts you might want to convey in the language of flowers.

1. **Good luck in your new job; success to you.**
   Anemone (expectations)
   Sweet basil (good wishes)
   White dianthus (talent)
   Wheat (riches)

2. **You are my secret love.**
   Forget-me-not (true love)
   Yellow acacia (secret love)

3. <u>You have wronged someone; curses on you.</u>
   Crocus (abuse not)
   Yellow rose (decreased love)
   Yellow carnation (disdain)

4. <u>I miss you.</u>
   Zinnia (thoughts of an absent friend)

5. <u>Happy birthday; long life.</u>
   Hyacinth (game, play)
   Yellow lily (gaiety)
   Stock (lasting beauty)

6. <u>Thank you; you are a true friend.</u>
   Oakland geranium (true friendship)
   Sage (esteem)
   Ranunculus (rich in attractions)

7. <u>Welcome to the new arrival.</u>
   White rosebud (babyhood)
   Daisy (innocence)
   White lilac (youthful innocence)

8. <u>I love you; happy anniversary.</u>
   Red tulips (declaration)
   Bridal rose (happy love)

Flowers for Arrangements

*T*he charts on the pages that follow outline my favorite flowers for arranging. All flowers—whether cultivated or wild—will survive with nothing more than a container filled with fresh water. But why not prolong the pleasure and luxury they provide by spending a few extra moments in preparing them for display? If you follow the standard preparation and conditioning techniques set forth on pages 197-200, you can extend the vase-life of your flowers considerably. Those flowers that might benefit with special treatment are dealt with individually in the "Useful Comments" column of the charts.

The key points to remember in preparing flowers for arrangements are as follows:

★ Cut stems on an angle with a sharp knife.
★ Remove all below-water-level foliage to retard decay.
★ Always place flowers in tepid water.
★ Keep your containers scrupulously clean. Residue from previous arrangements encourages bacteria growth.
★ Before arranging, condition flower stems and branches by giving them a long, deep, and restful drink of water. This is to allow them time to absorb as much water as possible into their capillary system. The water "hardens" the stems and strengthens the flower heads—insurance against drooping and wilting.
★ After you have completed your arrangement, keep the water in the container fresh. If possible, change it every day. Otherwise, add a few drops of household bleach to the water to delay the growth of harmful bacteria.

Common Name	Botanical Name	When to Cut or Buy	Color	Useful Comments
Achillea (Yarrow)	*Achillea millefolium*	In full bloom	Mustard-yellow	Cut stem, strip foliage, and condition in tepid water. ● Excellent for dried arrangements (hang upside down to dry). ● Lasts 1 week in water.
Agapanthus (African lily; Lily of the Nile)	*Agapanthus umbellatus*	Some flowers in full bloom, others unopened	Blue Violet Cream White	Adds drama and height to large arrangements. ● Hang seed head down to dry. ● Lasts 1 week in water.
Alchemilla (Lady's mantle)	*Alchemilla vulgaris*	In full bloom	Yellowish green	Hang upside down to dry. ● Lasts 1 week in water.
Allium	*Allium*	In full bloom, with compact flower heads	Blue violet Pink Rose Yellow White	To remove onion odor, add 1 teaspoon bleach to full vase water. ● Effective accent in large arrangements. ● Lasts 1 week in water.
Alstroemeria (Peruvian lily)	*Alstroemeria pelegrina*	Blossoms slightly open	White Pink Mauve Yellow Coral	Strip lower foliage, trim stem, and harden in water solution of ¼ teaspoon bleach and 1 teaspoon sugar. ● Long graceful stem attractive in tall arrangements. ● Lasts 1 to 2 weeks in water.

212

Common Name	Botanical Name	When to Cut or Buy	Color	Useful Comments
Amaranth (Globe amaranth)	*Gomphrena globosa*	In full bloom	Purplish blue Pink White Yellow Orange	Cut and slit stem; remove lower foliage and place in tepid water. ● Button shape adds delicate accent to bouquets. ● Hang upside down in bunches to dry. ● Lasts 5 to 7 days.
Amaryllis (Belladonna lily)	*Hippeastrum reginae*	Blossoms slightly open and fragrant; winter blooming	Apricot Pink White Red	Condition in deep water. Add 1 teaspoon peppermint oil to 1 quart water for longer lasting bloom. For professional treatment, fill stems with water and plug ends with cotton (see page 199). ● Lasts 1 week in water.
Anemone (Windflower)	*Anemone coronaria*	Tight bud (opens in warm room)	Blue Purple White Pink Fuchsia	Gently scrape lower 2 inches of stem. Condition in 1 cup vinegar to 1 quart water. To harden, set up to neck in water in a cool, dark place. ● Lasts 5 to 7 days in water, if kept cool. Does not last long in green foam.
Anthurium (Flamingo flower; Painted tongue)	*Anthurium*	Tropical plant available year round through florists	Red White Coral Cream	Cut stem on angle and place in tepid water. Support head on side of container. Wire stem for greater strength. ● An exotic flower with a sturdy stem that lends itself to modern, oriental and high-style arrangements. ● Lasts up to 2 weeks.
Aster (China aster)	*Callistephus hortensis*	In full bloom	Lavender Blue Pink Rose White	Break (don't cut) and smash stem. Scrape lower 2 inches. Condition in 1 teaspoon sugar per quart water. Before hardening, wire stem to support head. ● Lasts 7 to 10 days in water.

213

Common Name		Botanical Name	When to Cut or Buy	Color	Useful Comments
Astilbe		*Astilbe rivularis*	In full bloom	Pink Red Lavender White	Cut stems, smash or split ends, and place in tepid water. ● Airy accent to mass arrangements. ● Dries well. ● Lasts 2 weeks in water.
Azalea		*Rhododendron ponticum*	Blossoms slightly open	Pink White	Smash base of woody stem with hammer. Condition in 1 tablespoon rubbing alcohol per gallon water. ● Lasts 1 week in water.
Baby's breath		*Gypsophila paniculata*	In full bloom; year round	White Pink	Condition in 1 teaspoon rubbing alcohol to 1 pint water before arranging. ● Delicate, lacy accent for wedding bouquets and mass arrangements. ● Dries well in a little water or hung up to dry. ● Lasts at least 2 weeks in water.
Bachelor's button (Cornflower)		*Centaurea cyanus*	In full bloom; summer	Blue Pink White	Color of flower should be rich when picked; fading indicates age. ● Condition in deep water. If stem is weak, insert wire through center of flower down to base. Cut off dead shoots to promote secondary bloom. ● Lasts 5 days in water.
Bell Flower		*Campanula persicifolia*	In bud and bloom	Blue Lavender White Pink	Smash or split stem. Singe or boil end. Condition in tepid water before arranging. ● Lasts 1 to 2 weeks in water.

214

Common Name	Botanical Name	When to Cut or Buy	Color	Useful Comments
Bells of Ireland	*Moluccella laevis*	When green bell-shaped calycles open; late summer	Chartreuse	Crush stems before hardening in tepid water. • Gives line and height to tall arrangements. • Lasts up to 10 days in water.
Bird-of-paradise	*Strelitzia reginae*	Tropical plant available year round through florists	Orange and blue	Condition before arranging in water with ½ cup vinegar. Harden. Prolong display life with floral additive and frequent changes of water. • Showy display flower effective in large arrangements. • Lasts 7 to 12 days in water.
Bittersweet	*Solanum dulcamara*	Berries firm, some still yellow; in early fall	Orange	Smash or split stem; peel bark back 2 inches and place in tepid water. • Ornamental woody vine with clusters of small orange-red berries. Effective accent in fall arrangements. Hardy and long-lasting. • Lasts over 2 weeks in water.
Buttercup (Kingcup)	*Ranunculus acris*	Pick early or late in the day when buds open	Yellow	Place in tepid water immediately after cutting. • Charming wild flower for casual country arrangements. • Fragile. Lasts 2 days at best.
Butterfly weed	*Asclepias tuberosa*	Orange buds mixed with green	Orange	Place in tepid water immediately after picking. • Hardy, long-lasting summer wild flower. • Lasts 10 days in water.

Common Name		Botanical Name	When to Cut or Buy	Color	Useful Comments
Calla lily		*Calla palustris*	Buds ready to open or unfurled bloom; early summer	White Cream Yellow Pink	Condition overnight in deep water (leaves included), with solution of ½ cup vinegar to every 1 quart water. Wire head for added support. ● Effective focal flower for tall massed arrangements; also dramatic in high-style and oriental displays. ● Lasts 5 to 7 days in water.
Camellia		*Camellia japonica*	In bud or barely open; fall to spring	White Red Pink Rose	Prepare by smashing or splitting branch and placing in warm shallow water. To float, keep water off petals. Do not mist. To keep a camellia bloom lasting longer, put 1 teaspoon water in a brandy snifter. Place bloom in glass and cover with plastic wrap. ● Noted for its brilliant waxy foliage; effective in formal arrangements. ● Lasts 2 to 5 days in water.
Candytuft		*Iberus amara*	In slight bloom; early summer	White Pink Lavender Mauve	Smash or split stem, remove foliage below water level, and place in tepid water. ● Pungent odor. Winged and notched pod head adds a beautiful crisp accent to arrangements. ● Seed head dries well. ● Lasts 5 to 7 days in water.
Canterbury bell		*Campanula medium*	In slight bloom; late spring	Blue White Rose	Cut stem and burn end. Harden in tepid water. ● Lasts 1 week in water.
Carnation		*Dianthus caryophyllus*	In full bloom, head firm	Yellow White Pink Red Mauve Apricot Bicolored	Trim lower foliage and cut on slant below stem node. Split larger stems. Tight buds will open faster if conditioned first in warm, not tepid, water. ● Lasts 7 to 10 days in water.

Common Name	Botanical Name	When to Cut or Buy	Color	Useful Comments
Cattail (Reed mace, club rush)	*Typha latifolia*	Flowers dark and firm; end of summer	Brown	Remove foliage and cut to desired length. Soak in cool water. ● Excellent accent for height and preserved-flower arrangements.
Chrysanthemum (Shasta daisy, pompom, spider or Fuji, daisy mums, others)	*Chrysanthemum morifolium*	In full bloom, centers should not be brown	Yellow White Red Purple others	Break or smash stems and scrape ends with knife. Remove all foliage below water level. Condition in deep water 24 hours. A few drops of peppermint oil prolongs vase life. ● Lasts up to 2 weeks in water. Recondition if necessary.
Clover	*Trifolium*	Tight buds with color showing	Purple Red White	Needs water as soon as possible after picking. ● Lasts 1 week in water.
Cockscomb Amaranth (Brainflower)	*Celosia cristata*	Firm, showing good color; fall bloom	Red Pink Yellow Orange	Smash or split stems and place in warm water to harden. ● Dramatic, large flower head adds bold form to mass arrangements. Effective main element when displayed in narrow container. ● Air dry by hanging upside down. ● Lasts 10 days in water.
Coneflower (Black-eyed Susan)	*Rudbeckia*	Petals looking up; firm center	Yellow, with a dark center	Split stems and immerse in cool water containing sugar for 1 to 2 hours before arranging. Remove leaves as soon as they begin to wilt. ● Lasts 1 to 2 weeks in water.

217

Common Name		Botanical Name	When to Cut or Buy	Color	Useful Comments
Coreopsis (Tickseed)		*Coreopsis tinctoria*	In full bloom before pollen forms	Yellow Crimson Maroon	Cut stems and place in deep tepid water. Delicate blossom—may not absorb water. ● Prolific summer wild flower that also thrives under cultivation. ● Lasts 1 to 2 weeks in water.
Crocus		*Crocus*	Bud slightly open; early spring	Purple Blue Yellow Pink White	Cut stem gently above white bulb part of stem. Rinse under cold water and place in tepid water. ● Delicate spring accent for mixed arrangements. Lovely in assorted bud vases. ● Lasts up to 3 days in water.
Daffodil		*Narcissus biflorus*	In bud stage	Yellow White Orange Bicolored	Cut off white part of stem and slit. Rinse off sap under cold running water. Harden in shallow cool water overnight. Mist frequently after arranging. ● Lasts 4 to 6 days in water.
Dahlia		*Dahlia variabilis*	In bloom, with crisp petals	Various	Remove foliage below water level. Cut stem on diagonal and slit vertically to increase water flow. To condition, singe stem or dip in boiling water, then place in tepid water with ¼ cup vinegar per quart water for 1 hour. Soak in separate container with fresh water to harden. ● Lasts 5 to 7 days in water.
Daisy (Marguerite)		*Chrysanthemum frutescens*	In full bloom, petals facing upward	White Yellow	Remove all foliage below water level. Cut stem on angle with knife, scrape base. Singe or dip stem end in boiling water. Place in deep water with ¼ teaspoon peppermint oil. Flower additive and frequent changes of water prolong vase life. ● Lasts 10 days in water.

Common Name	Botanical Name	When to Cut or Buy	Color	Useful Comments
Dandelion (Lion's tooth)	*Taraxacum officinale*	In full bloom	Yellow	Unless ends are singed before conditioning, it will not do well in arrangements. ● Lasts 3 to 5 days in water.
Day lily	*Hemerocallis fulva*	In bloom with some blossoms in bud form	Orange Yellow Copper Bicolored	Each blossom on the stem lasts one day but is replaced by developing buds on successive days. To make flower open at night, try storing the stem in a bucket of cool water in a dark place during the day. ● Lasts up to 14 days in water.
Delphinium (Larkspur)	*Delphinium exaltatum*	When not more than half the flowers on stalk are open	Blue Purple White Pink Mauve	Cut stem diagonally and slit hollow base to increase water flow. Pierce stem just below flower head with pin to allow trapped air bubbles to escape. ● Lasts 1 week in water.
Dill	*Peucedanum graveolens*	Before reaching full bloom	Yellowish green	Condition in tepid water. ● Soft, airy accent for mixed arrangements. ● Lasts up to 2 weeks in water.
Dock (Sorrel)	*Rumex crispus*	Flower greenish brown and firm	Brown	Smash stem and place in warm water. ● Takes well to drying upside down.

Common Name		Botanical Name	When to Cut or Buy	Color	Useful Comments
Dogwood		*Cornus sanguinea*	Early blossom or in bud, showing color; mid-spring	White Pink Rose Variegated	Break and hammer stem. Peel off 2 inches of bark from stem. To force, soak in deep warm water overnight or longer before arranging. Stir in a few drops bleach and sugar additive to container water; change water solution and recondition every few days. ● Lasts 8 to 10 days in water.
Dusty miller		*Centaurea gymnocarpa*	Foliage unblemished; summer	Silver foliage	Strip leaves below water level off stem. ● Excellent filler for low arrangement. ● Hang upside down to dry. ● Last 2 weeks in water.
Eremurus (Foxtail lily)		*Eremurus*	Flower head partially open; early summer	Yellow Peach White Pink	Cut stem and place in tepid water. ● Spiked flower spectacular in tall arrangements. ● Lasts 10 days in water.
Euphorbia (Spurge)		*Euphorbia*	Flowers and buds open. No brown edges; early spring	Yellow White Red Orange Pink	Cut stem, rinse off milky sap. Remove short leaves surrounding florets. Singe or boil stem ends. Place immediately in tepid water to harden. ● Same family as Poinsettia. Long stem adds elegant line to large arrangements. ● Lasts 1 week in water.
Fern		*Filices* (many genera and species)	Foliage crisp and green, not brown, yellow, or shedding	Green, various shades	Harden completely covered with cold water. May be stored in box or plastic bag in cool place for long periods. Keep moist when storing. ● Filler for flower arrangements (see Foliage chart, page 196). ● Lasts 2 to 3 weeks in water.

Common Name	Botanical Name	When to Cut or Buy	Color	Useful Comments
Forget-me-not	*Myosotis palustris*	Flower beginning to open	Blue White Pink	Cut stem and place in cool water. If stem wilts, dip ends in boiling water quickly and refresh in cold water. ● Delicate addition to small nosegays. ● Lasts 5 to 7 days in water.
Forsythia	*Forsythia*	Flowers beginning to open; early spring, for forcing, late winter	Yellow White	Before placing in water, cut and smash stems with hammer. Peel lower two inches from bottom and slit stem. ● To force bloom, place in very warm water with a few drops of ammonia. Cover container tightly with plastic. Flowers will open in 24 hours. Transfer to fresh water; add floral preservative or sugar. ● Lasts 1 to 2 weeks in water.
Foxglove	*Digitalis*	Up to half the flowers on stem partially open; early summer	White Yellow Pinkish purple Yellow	Cut stem diagonally under warm water. Smash heavier stems. For professional preconditioning, fill stems with water and plug with cotton (see page 199). ● Tall spike flower effective accent for mixed arrangements. ● Lasts 5 to 10 days in water.
Freesia	*Freesia*	The first flowers on each stem open	Yellow White Blue Lavender Pink Red	Cut stem diagonally under tepid water. Before arranging, harden overnight in water treated with sugar or floral food additive. Remove lower blooms as they wilt. ● Fragrant and graceful accent to bouquets and mass arrangements. ● Lasts 5 to 10 days in water.
Geranium	*Geranium* or *Pelargonium*	Flower clusters in bud and showing color	Red Pink Purple White Salmon variegated	Remove leaves below water level from stems and place in tepid water. When cut, foliage with greens will continue to grow and establish root system, suitable for transplanting. ● Excellent filler for summer bouquets. ● Lasts 5 to 7 days in water.

Common Name	Botanical Name	When to Cut or Buy	Color	Useful Comments
Gerbera (African daisy; Transvaal)	*Gerbera*	In full bloom, with crisp petals	Pink Scarlet Orange Coral Yellow Cream	Cut and split stems. Singe or boil ends for 15 seconds before hardening overnight in deep tepid water containing sugar or floral preservative. ● Heads frequently need support. ● Colorful choice for tall containers. ● Lasts up to 3 weeks in water.
Gladiolus	*Gladiolus communis*	2 to 3 blossoms on the stem, barely open	Yellow Purple White Red Orange Salmon	Cut and split stems under running water. Pinch off green-budded tips to encourage all buds to open. Soak in deep tepid water containing sugar or floral additive. ● Handsome, tall flower for large arrangements. ● Lasts up to 2 weeks in treated water.
Goldenrod	*Solidago virgaurea*	Flower pale green, before pollen forms; July to August	Pale green immature, golden yellow mature	Cut stems, remove foliage and soak in tepid water. ● Colorful accent for bouquets of summer garden flowers. ● Dries well by tying loosely in bunches and hanging upside down.
Grape, wild (Muscadine grape)	*Vitis rotundifolia*	Vine supple, not dried	Brown stems, green leaves	Soak in deep water overnight before molding. ● Use for linear accents in arrangements as well as wreaths. ● Long-lasting.
Grass (Cloud; Elephant; Quaking; Timothy; Walking stick; others)	*Gramineae*	Year round	Green Brown Golden	Place in tepid water. ● Grasses add long, graceful curves and texture to massed arrangements. ● To air dry, tie loosely in bunches and stand upright in tall container.

Common Name		Botanical Name	When to Cut or Buy	Color	Useful Comments
Heather (Scotch heather)		*Calluna vulgaris*	Young blooms; early fall	Lavender Pink Purple White	Break and split stem. Hairspray applied to flower holds bloom and preserves color. Stand upright in shallow water to condition before arranging. ● Lasts 1 to 2 weeks in water.
Heliconia (Lobster claw)		*Heliconia*	Select stem with mostly developed blossoms and some buds showing color	Red Yellow	To condition, recut stem on an angle and immerse in tepid water. ● Dramatic tropical plant for high-style and "abstract" arrangements.
Holly		*Ilex*	Shiny, green leaves and hard, bright red berries; winter	Green, variegated	Smash stems and scrape off bark at ends with a knife. Condition in tepid water. ● Lasts several weeks in water.
Hollyhock		*Althaea rosea*	Blossoms formed	Pink Red White Yellow Blue Lavender	Cut stems on slant, remove all leaves, and smash or split stem end before singeing 15 seconds. Condition in deep tepid water with ½ cup salt for two hours. Transfer to pail of plain water to harden overnight. ● Lasts 2 to 5 days in water.
Honeysuckle		*Lonicera periclymenum*	Spring blossoming vine	Pale yellow White Pink	Scrape off outer bark at ends, split or smash stems and place in tepid water. ● To force bloom as soon as buds show color, cut vine and submerge in warm water containing 1 tablespoon ammonia. Cover container with plastic overnight. The next day transfer to container filled with cool water. Mist often. ● Lasts 7 to 10 days in water.

Common Name	Botanical Name	When to Cut or Buy	Color	Useful Comments
Hyacinth	*Hyacinthus orientalis*	Blossoms beginning to open at base of stalk but tight buds at top; early spring	Lavender Pink White Yellow Blue	Before arranging, cut off white part of stem, rinse under running water, and place in cold water 1 hour to allow sap to drain. ● If wilting occurs, dip end in boiling water or singe for a few seconds, then refresh in tepid water. ● Lasts 1 week in water.
Hydrangea	*Hydrangea hortensia*	In full bloom; summer	White Blue Red Pink	Remove most foliage. Scrape off bark from bottom inch of stem, smash or cross split end, and singe or boil stem 15 seconds. If flower begins to wilt, plunge head in water for a minute, shake off excess, and place stem in deep water to harden overnight. ● To dry, stand in shallow container and let water evaporate. ● Fresh flower lasts 7 to 12 days in water.
Iris	*Iris*	First bud on stalk ready to open, color showing	White Orange Yellow Blue Purple Mauve Others	Cut stem on angle and condition in 2 tablespoons salt to 1 quart tepid water for 1 to 2 hours. Harden in water solution containing sugar or floral preservative. ● Iris doesn't like temperature changes: keep away from heat, drafts, and sun. ● Lasts a few days.
Ixia	*Ixia*	Blossoms beginning to open	Orange Pink	Cut stems on diagonal and place in tepid water. ● Lasts 1 week in water.
Lady Slipper (Moccasin flower)	*Cypripedium*	Spring (endangered species)	Pink Variegated greens Lavender	Mottled leaf variety of the orchid family. ● Best purchased as a flowering house plant.

Common Name	Botanical Name	When to Cut or Buy	Color	Useful Comments
Lavender	*Lavandula officinalis*	Flowers showing color and not shedding	Purple Pale Lavender Pink White	Smash or split stem. Condition in cool water. ● Fragrant. ● May be dried by hanging upside down in a dry place. ● Lasts 1 to 2 weeks in water.
Liatris (Blazing star; Gay feather)	*Liatris spicata*	Spike buds showing color; summer	Purple Lavender	Cut stem and smash or slit end. Place in cool water to condition. ● To dry, stand upright. ● Lasts 7 to 10 days in water.
Lilac	*Syringa vulgaris*	Clusters almost in full bloom; spring	Purple White Pink	Remove all leaves except near head. Peel off bark two inches from base. Crush or slit stem; thoroughly mist flower heads and condition stems in deep, cool water overnight. ● Lasts 5 to 7 days in water.
Lily	*Lilium*	Stalk with some closed buds and several open flowers	All colors except blue	Cut stem on diagonal and remove foliage below water level. Place in deep, cool water to condition thoroughly. Do not mist flower and beware of pollen; it stains. Removing anthers prevents pollen from falling on furniture and fabric. ● Lasts 10 to 14 days.
Lily of the Valley	*Convallaria majalis*	Top buds on stalk closed, lower blossoms in full bloom; late spring	White	If taken from garden, cut and place in water for a few hours. If greenhouse bought, wrap in tissue and place in shallow, warm water for 1 hour. Add additional water and let stand to condition overnight. ● Lasts 3 to 5 days.

Common Name	Botanical Name	When to Cut or Buy	Color	Useful Comments
Lupine	*Lupinus*	Flowering stalk still partially in bud; late spring	Blue Purple Rose White	Remove foliage and cut stems diagonally; then split ends. Allow stems to fill with water and plug ends with cotton (optional). ● Lasts 5 to 7 days in water.
Marigold (French and African)	*Tagetes*	Centers should be tight and firm, showing true color; early fall	Yellow Gold Orange Maroon Red Cream	Cut on slant, remove all foliage, and scrape stems with a knife. Let stand several hours in deep, tepid water containing a few drops of peppermint oil. ● Lasts 7 to 10 days in water.
Mimosa (Acacia)	*Mimosa* or *Acacia*	Blossoms on tree fluffy; early summer	Yellow Pink	Condition by smashing branches with hammer and placing in warm water. ● Blossom and foliage may be dried for long-lasting arrangements. ● Lasts 2 to 3 days in water.
Mistletoe	*Viscum album*	Foliage fresh and berries on stem	White berries and grey-green foliage	Smash stem and place in warm water. ● Traditional Christmas decoration.
Mock Orange	*Philadelphus coronarius*	Some flowers partially open, others still in bud; late spring	White and yellow	Smash stem. Strip most foliage. Condition in deep water. ● Long, graceful branches are effective for line and color in mixed arrangements and singly. ● May be forced in early spring. ● Lasts 7 to 10 days in water.

Common Name	Botanical Name	When to Cut or Buy	Color	Useful Comments
Monkshood	*Aconitum napellus*	Flowers beginning to open; summer	Blue White Purple Violet	Cut stem and place in tepid water. ● Lasts 1 week in water.
Montbretia	*Crocosmia aurea*	Buds on end of spike closed, with several flowers unfurled; summer	Orange Scarlet	Cut stem and place in tepid water. ● Lasts 1 week in water.
Mustard	*Brassica*	In full bloom before petals start to darken; summer wild flower	Yellow-gold	Cut and place in tepid water. ● Hang upside down to dry.
Narcissus	*Narcissus poeticus*	Buds opening; early spring	White with yellow center	Cut stem at an angle and slit. Stand in deep, cool water one hour before arranging. ● Lasts 4 to 6 days in water.
Nasturtium	*Tropaeolum majus*	Flowers in advanced bud stage; summer blooming container plant	Orange Gold Crimson	Cut stems and place in cool water. ● Brilliant color makes this an unusual accent flower for subtle arrangements. ● Lasts 4 to 5 days in water.

Common Name		Botanical Name	When to Cut or Buy	Color	Useful Comments
Nerine		*Nerine*	In full bloom	Hot pink Red Crimson	Cut stem and place in tepid water. ● Excellent winter accent flower for adding color, height, and line to mixed arrangements. ● This relative newcomer to floral fashion is imported from Holland and widely available year round. ● Lasts 7 to 10 days in water.
Orchid		*Orchis*	In full bloom, fleshy, thick, and waxy	Varied	Cut stem on a slant and place in cool water. Keeps well in refrigerator if covered with plastic to retain moisture. ● Spectacular in floral design as well as to wear. ● Of the 25,000 known species, all are either *Epiphytic* (grown on trees; their roots clinging to bark) or *Terrestrial* (grown in the ground).
Pansy		*Viola tricolor*	Flowers open, petals turning up	Varied	Cut stems and place in cool water. Not long lasting in green foam. ● Lasts three to four days.
Peony		*Paeonia officinalis*	Blossoms almost closed, showing color	Pink White Rose Magenta Yellow	Condition leaves separately, cut stems, slit ends, and place in cool or warm water. ● Remove all foliage and reserve to condition leaves separately. Smash or split stems and float flower head and stem in deep cool water for 2 to 3 hours. Arrange in water containing 3 tablespoons sugar per quart water or a generous supply of floral additive. ● Lasts 1 week in water.
Phlox		*Phlox*	Flowers slightly open; summer	White Pink Crimson Lavender Blue	Cut below stem joint, and remove lower foliage. Condition in cool water overnight.

228

Common Name	Botanical Name	When to Cut or Buy	Color	Useful Comments
Pinks	*Dianthus deltoides*	In full bloom, with leaves firm and crisp	White Pink Rose Mauve Red Bicolored	Trim lower foliage and cut a slant below leaf node. Harden in tepid water (use warmer water if you need to force buds to open more quickly). Add sugar solution or flower additive to water in arrangement. ● The Miniature carnation is a versatile flower for small "country style" bouquets. At its best in groupings of bud vases on the table. ● Lasts 7 to 10 days in water.
Poinsettia	*Euphorbia pulcherrima*	Available as potted plant; early winter	Red Pink White Variegated	Singe or boil the stem. Rub salt into burned end and harden in cold water. Avoid drafts and direct sun. ● Lasts 4 to 5 days in water.
Poppy	*Papaver orientale*	Tight blossom; late spring	Pink Red Orange White	Cut on angle and singe or boil stem. Rub salt into burned end and harden in cold water containing sugar or floral additive. ● Lasts 3 to 5 days in water.
Protea	*Protea*	Petals open and firm	White Cream Rose Pink Coral Bicolored	Cut and split or smash stem. Remove foliage. Singe or dip ends in boiling water 15 seconds; then soak in tepid water to harden. ● Lasts about 2 weeks in water.
Pussy willow	*Salix discolor*	When buds or catkins have begun to develop; late winter	Pinkish gray	Split stem and scrape off 1 to 2 inches bark at stem end. Place in tepid water. Excellent for forcing. ● Lasts 2 to 3 weeks in water.

Common Name	Botanical Name	When to Cut or Buy	Color	Useful Comments
Queen Anne's Lace (wild carrot)	*Daucus carota*	Lacy blossom white-green and showing no signs of shedding. August, early fall	White Pale green Pale pink	Condition in tepid water. Soft, airy accent for arrangements. ● Dries well standing upright. ● Lasts 5 days in water.
Ranunculus (buttercup)	*Ranunculus asiaticus*	In early bloom; late spring	Yellow Orange White Rose Red	Split stems and dip ends in boiling water, then harden in cool tepid water. ● Lasts 1 to 2 weeks in water.
Rose	*Rosa*	In bud or slightly open	All colors except blue	With a sharp knife cut off foliage and thorns while the stems are in water. Cut stems on the diagonal. To revive wilted heads, recut and slit ends and float in cool water overnight. Use floral additive to nurture blossoms and retard bacteria growth. Change water and add new additive daily. ● Most will last from 3 to 7 days in water.
Snapdragon	*Antirrhinum majus*	Lower flowers on stalk in full bloom, top in bud	White Pink Red Orange Yellow	With stems under water, remove foliage and cut ends at an angle. Plunge stems in deep warm water for one hour before arranging. Wilted snaps benefit from singeing or boiling water treatment. ● Lasts 1 week in water.
Snowball	*Virburnum trilobum*	Blossoms white and formed; early spring	White	Remove most foliage, smash stems, and place in tepid water. ● Lasts 1 week in water.

Common Name	Botanical Name	When to Cut or Buy	Color	Useful Comments
Snowdrop	*Galanthus nivalis*	Leaves firm, berries hard and white; early spring	White	Cut and smash stems and place in tepid water. • Lasts 1 week in water.
Star of Bethlehem (Chincherinchee)	*Ornithogalum umbellatum*	Top buds closed, bottom blossoms open	White Greenish-white Cream	Condition by cutting stem above white base at a sharp angle and placing in tepid water. Remove old blossoms as they wither. Change water often and recut stems every 5 days. • This flower, which is readily available at florists year round, closes at night and is an excellent accent for mixed arrangements. • Lasts 3 weeks in water.
Statice (Sea lavender)	*Limonium vulgare*	Flowers fully formed and showing good color; pick in dry weather	Lavender Blue White Pink Yellow	Cut end and scrape off outer green ridge along lower stem. Place in tepid water. • May be dried. • Lasts 2 to 3 weeks.
Stock	*Matthiola*	When half of the blossoms on a stem are open	Cream Pink Lavender Purple Red Yellow	Split stem and remove all foliage except near flower head. Harden overnight in cold water containing 1 tablespoon sugar and 2 tablespoons white vinegar per quart water. • Wonderfully fragrant. Excellent for mixed arrangements.
Sweet pea	*Lathyrus odoratus*	Some blossoms open and unblemished, stems firm; spring, early summer	White Cream Pink Purple Red Orange	Cut stems and condition in very shallow, tepid water containing 1 tablespoon sugar. Avoid wetting petals. • Delicate, clear blossom makes this an excellent flower for soft accents in arrangements. • Lasts 5 to 8 days in water.

Common Name	Botanical Name	When to Cut or Buy	Color	Useful Comments
Sweet William	*Dianthus barbatus*	In full bloom	Pink Red Rose Purple White Bicolored	Cut stem in water below joint and place in tepid water containing 1 tablespoon rubbing alcohol for 1 hour. Then soak in cool water before arranging. ● This flower is rich in color and long-lasting. ● Lasts 7 to 12 days in water.
Tansy (Buttons)	*Tanacetum vulgare*	Stems with both flowers and buds	White Yellow	Grows wild on roadsides and sandy wasteland. ● Cut and place in tepid water, removing foliage below water level. ● Dries well. ● Lasts 5 to 7 days in water.
Teasel (Fuller's teasel)	*Dipsacus fullonum*	Color will stay lighter if picked before flower is in full bloom; July	Brown	Remove leaves and prickles; cut and place in tepid water. ● Good delicate accent and filler for fresh and dried arrangements. ● Air dry in loose bunches standing upright. ● Lasts 1 week in water.
Tuberose	*Polianthes tuberosa*	In full bloom; summer	White Cream	Cut stem and place in tepid water for one hour before arranging. ● Lovely fragrance. ● Lasts 1 week in water.
Tulip	*Tulipa*	Buds bursting	Various Bicolored	With stem in water, remove lower foliage and side shoots. Cut stem on the diagonal above white base. Wrap a tight tube of wax paper or other non-absorbent paper around a bunch of blossoms, enabling heads to stay erect. Stand tube in deep, cool water overnight to harden. ● To prolong vase life, add 1 teaspoon sugar and decay retardant to container. ● Lasts up to 1 week in water.

Common Name	Botanical Name	When to Cut or Buy	Color	Useful Comments
Veronica	*Veronica*	Flowers showing color; early summer	White Pink Blue Purple	Cut stem and place in tepid water. ● Long-lasting and effective in summer arrangements. ● Lasts 1 week in water.
Violet	*Viola odorata*	Flowers beginning to open	Purple White	Let stand in icy water up to the neck one hour before arranging. Delicate stem; do not use in green foam. ● Pretty when bunched and surrounded by own foliage. ● Lasts 4 to 7 days in water.
Waxplant (Hoya)	*Hoya carnosa*	Flowers opening on vine with some buds	Pink White	Smash stems and place in tepid water. ● Lovely lemon fragrance. ● Lasts 7 days in water.
Witch hazel	*Hamamelis virginiana*	Stems with buds; late winter	Golden yellow flower; black stem	Smash branch ends and place in warm water. ● Adds height and grace to tall arrangements. ● Effective in dried arrangements. ● Lasts 5 to 7 days in water.
Zinnia	*Zinnia elegans*	In full bloom with tight centers	Various; no blue	Remove bottom leaves and side shoots. Condition stems in boiling water for 1 minute, then place in cool water up to the neck to harden. ● To prevent head from breaking stem, insert wire through blossom into stem. ● Lasts one week or more in water.

Resource Guide

Rentals, Equipment & Supplies

California

Regal Rents
9925 Jefferson Boulevard
Culver City, CA 90230
213-204-3382

San Francisco Party Rentals
848 Folsom Street
San Francisco, CA 94107
415-864-4905

Connecticut

Table Toppers
103 Briar Brae Road
Stamford, CT
203-329-9977

Illinois

HDO Productions, Inc.
237 Melvin Drive
Northbrook, IL 60062
312-564-1700
*Tents of every size and shape;
delivery anywhere in USA*

Iowa

Blackhawk Films, Inc.
1 Old Eagle Brewery
Box 3990
Davenport, IA 52808
319-323-9736

New Jersey

Party Rentals Ltd.
400 North Street
Teterboro, NJ 07608
212-594-8510;
301-984-0963
*Relied on by party profession-
als; will ship anywhere*

New York

House of Costumes
166 Jericho Turnpike
Mineola, NY 11501
516-294-0170
Costumes, masks, wigs, etc.

Films Incorporated
440 Park Avenue South
New York, NY 10016
800-223-6246;
212-889-7910

Frost Lighting
Box 489, FDR Station
New York, NY 10150
212-751-0223
*Outdoor and indoor lighting;
other offices in Chicago,
West Palm Beach, Washing-
ton D.C., and Wilmington*

Service Party Rental
521 E. 72nd Street
New York, NY 10021
212-288-7384

Tenth House Enterprises
P.O. Box 810
Gracie Station
New York, NY 10028
212-737-7536
*Space location service for special
events*

Times Square Lighting
318 W. 47th Street
New York, NY 10036
212-541-5045
*Indoor special effects and disco
lighting; rentals and sales*

Tennessee

Party and Rental Services,
Inc.
277 White Bridge Road
Nashville, TN 37209
615-356-4501

Caterers

Alabama

Homer L. McClure Catering
Services
208 S. Catherine Street
Mobile, AL 36604
205-473-2151

Arizona

Avanti Caterers of Distinction
3102 N. Scottsdale Road
Scottsdale, AZ 85251
602-956-0926

C. Steele & Co.—Market
Place
7422 E. Indian School Road
Scottsdale, AZ 85251
602-994-0755

California

Forks & Fingers
Del Marin Keys Boulevard
Suite M
Novato, CA 94947
415-883-1900

The Butler Did It
3595 Las Pampas Way
Palm Springs, CA 92264
619-323-5799

Edible Art
758 Clementina Street
San Francisco, CA 94103
415-751-2129

Fred Wertheim
3421 Jackson Street
San Francisco, CA 94118
415-921-8970

Taste Catering Inc.
55 Rodgers Street
San Francisco, CA 94103
415-864-4321

Rococo Catering
6412 Independence Avenue
Woodland Hills, CA 91367
213-348-1574

Colorado

Panache
1579 S. Pearl
Denver, CO 80210
303-777-9620

Three Tomatoes Catering
  Kitchen
2019 E. 17th Avenue
Denver, CO 80206
303-393-7010

Connecticut

Cook's Corner
9 Sconset Square
Westport, CT 06880
203-227-9554

Martha Stewart, Inc.
48 S. Turkey Hill Road
Westport, CT 06880
203-255-1430

District of Columbia

B & B Catering
7041 Blair Road, NW
Washington, D.C. 20012
202-829-8640

Glorious Food
3251 Prospect Street, NW
Washington, D.C. 20007
202-342-0666

Florida

Gene's Catering Service, Inc.
8944 Northwest 24th Terrace
Miami, FL 33172
305-592-1311

Georgia

Affairs to Remember
680 Ponce de Leon Ave. NE
Atlanta, GA 30308
404-872-7859

The Company Co.
2301 Dellwood Drive
Atlanta, GA 30305
404-351-1875

Illinois

The Chicago Caterers
2901 N. Ashland Avenue
Chicago, IL 60657
312-975-8400

Gaper's Caterers
16 W. Washington Street
Chicago, IL 60602
312-332-4935

Patrick Collins
345 Fullerton Parkway
Chicago, IL 60614
312-871-1283

Kansas

Bonnie Shapiro
2008 W. 49th Terrace
Shawnee Mission, KS 66205
913-831-1164

Kentucky

La Pesche
1147 Bardstown Road
Louisville, KY 40204
502-451-0377

Maryland

Fiske Caterers
411 Coldspring Lane
Pikesville, MD 21208
301-235-6900

Massachusetts

Creative Gourmets Ltd.
1 Beacon Street
Boston, MA 02108
617-723-5555

Courrier & Chives
20 Tremont Street
Brighton, MA 02135
617-254-1112

Cuisine Chez Vous
650 Center Street
Newton, MA 21158
617-965-2456

The Catered Affair
333 Gannett Road
North Scituate, MA 02066
617-545-4742

Michigan

The Palate Pleaser
818 Bowers
Birmingham, MI 48008
313-540-2266

Rick's Glorious Foods
6646 Telegraph
Birmingham, MI 48010
313-855-4005

Gourmet House
25225 E. Jefferson
St. Claire Shores, MI 48081
313-771-0300

Merchant of Vino
29525 Northwestern
  Highway
Southfield, MI 48034
313-354-6505

Missouri

Robert Salsman & Associates
401 E. 31st
Kansas City, MO 64108
816-561-0266

Erker Catering Company
8066 Clayton Road
St. Louis, MO 63117
314-727-3366

Weinhardt Caterers
11601 Manchester Road
St. Louis, MO 63131
314-822-9000

Nebraska

Abraham Catering Service
1513 Military Avenue
Omaha, NB 68111
402-551-4410

Siegler's Catering Service
10737 Mockingbird Drive
Omaha, NB 68127
402-339-1410

New Mexico

Massee's
318 S. Guadaloupe Street
Sante Fe, NM 87501
505-983-5666

New York

Bespoke Food
311 E. 81st Street
New York, NY 10028
212-794-2248

Donald Bruce White, Inc.
159 E. 64th Street
New York, NY 10021
212-988-8410

Joseph J. M. Miller
315 E. 65th Street
New York, NY 10021
212-861-7923

Lars & Penates
95 Christopher Street
New York, NY 10014
212-242-4773

Lloyd Davis
82 E. 3rd Street
New York, NY 10003
212-244-4270

Mark Fahrer Catering
43 W. 13th Street
New York, NY 10011
212-243-6572

Nadine
27 E. 22nd Street
New York, NY 10011
212-838-2978

Victoria Campbell Kirsten
420 E. 72nd Street
New York, NY 10021
212-517-7766

North Carolina

Pat Benton
The Old Edwards Inn
Fourth & Main
Highlands, NC 28741
704-526-5036

Ohio

Cathi O'Brien
49 E. 4th Street
Cincinnatti, OH 45202
513-381-5999

Lenhardt Catering
4720 Eastern Avenue
Cincinnatti, OH 45226
513-321-8280

Oregon

Four & Twenty Blackbirds
455 2nd Street
Lake Oswego, OR 97231
503-635-4080

Eat Your Heart Out
831 NW 23rd
Portland, OR 97210
503-222-6111

Pennsylvania

Frog Commissary Catering
Service
117 S. 17th Street, Suite 2103
Philadelphia, PA 19103
215-569-2240

Rhode Island

Blackstone Caterers, Inc.
72 Ledge Street
Central Falls, RI 02863
401-724-8400

Michael's Personalized
Catering
748 Hope Street
Providence, RI 02920
401-421-9431

South Carolina

Cindy Porcher
300 Hobcaw Drive
Mount Pleasant, SC 29464
803-881-1911

Tennessee

Miss Daisy's Tea Room
Carters Court
Franklin, TN 37064
615-790-1934

Texas

Detterman's Catering
Company
5039 Willis
Dallas, TX 75260
214-821-6650

Epicure, Inc.
2156 W. Northwest Highway
Suite 312
Dallas, TX 75220
214-556-0660

Graham Catering
1947 W. Gray
Houston, TX 77019
713-526-0793

The Stock Pot
212½ N. High
Longview, TX 75606
214-753-6868

Catering by Don Strange
1551 Bandera Road
San Antonio, TX 78228
512-434-2331

Virginia

Annie Chalkley Pfoods, Etc.
Route 2, Box 89
Charles City, VA 23030
804-829-5248;
    804-272-8969

Gourmet Delight, Inc.
3158-B W. Cary Street
Richmond, VA 23221
804-358-7713

Party Pantry Inc.
119 N. Robinson Street
Richmond, VA 23220
804-353-8642

Washington

Gretchen's of Course
909 University
Seattle, WA 98101
206-623-8194

Mange Tout
1104 19th Avenue East
Seattle, WA 98112
206-329-1227

Market Place Caterers
94 Pike Street
Seattle, WA 98101
206-682-2208

Flower Designers

800 Flowers, Inc.
8001 Bent Branch Drive
Irving, TX 75063
800-356-9377
Nationwide flowers by toll-free phone service. Open every hour of the year. Delivered anywhere in the USA within 48 hours. Orders billed to credit-card number of caller.

Alabama

Park Lane Flowers
1911 Cahaba Road
Birmingham, AL 35223
205-879-7903

Arizona

Bob Branch Flowers
8645 N. 7th Street
Phoeniz, AZ 85020
602-264-2965

California

Flower Fashions
9960 Santa Monica Boulevard
Beverly Hills, CA 90212
213-275-0159

Dorothy Deming
2406 Sharon Oaks Drive
Menlowe Park, CA 94025
415-854-3122

Floridella
1920 Polk Street
San Francisco, CA 94109
415-775-4065

Green & Zlatonim
323 Prospect Avenue
San Francisco, CA 94110
415-641-8599

Colorado

Loop Flowers, Inc.
1510 California
Denver, CO 80202
303-629-1717;
    303-629-1776

Michael Jultak Florists, Inc.
5151 E. Colfax Avenue
Denver, CO 80220
303-388-6411

Connecticut

Nijole's Flowers by
    Nijole Valitis
104 Mason Street
Greenwich, CT 06830
203-661-1045

Country Flowers by
    Diana McDermott
25 Hanford Road
New Canaan, CT 06840

District of Columbia

Flowers of Georgetown
2300 Wisconsin Avenue, NW
Washington, D.C. 20007
202-333-3366

Nosegay Flower Shop, Inc.
1120 20th Street, NW
Washington, D.C. 20018
202-338-1146

Georgia

The Flower Lady
3311 Cains Hill Place
Atlanta, GA 30305
404-261-3551

Marvin Gardens Designs Ltd.
99 W. Paces Ferry Road NW
Atlanta, GA 30305
404-231-1988

Illinois

Jason Richards, Ltd.
42 E. Chicago Avenue
Chicago, IL 60611
312-664-0605

Ronsley, Inc.
363 W. Ontario Street
Chicago, IL 60610

McAdams Florists
810 S. Waukegan Road
Lake Forest, IL 60045
312-234-0625

Crest of Fine Flowers
417½ 4th
Wilmette, IL 60091
312-273-2282

Kansas

Legg Florist
5000 State Line
Kansas City, KS 66103
913-831-3022

Kentucky

Rod Wood, Florist
230 Holiday Manor
    Shopping Center
Louisville, KY 40222
502-425-5818

Maryland

Rowland Park Florist
Wyndhurst Avenue
Baltimore, MD 21210
301-435-2100

Massachusetts

Wildflowers Designs
227 Newberry Street
Boston, MA 02116
617-437-7779

Winston Flowers
131 Newberry Street
Boston, MA 02116
617-536-6861

The Dutch Garden
40 Brattle Street
Cambridge, MA 02138
617-491-0660

Michigan

Gary Flowers
415 E. Frank
Birmingham, MI 48238
313-642-2612

Jerry Earles Florist, Inc.
16851 James Couzens Fwy.
Detroit, MI 48238
313-341-9331

Kay Danzer
1301 W. Lafayette
Detroit, MI 48226
313-965-9030

Missouri

Richard V. Seaboldt
    Custom Florist
1417 W. 47th Street
Kansas City, MO 64112
816-561-9752

George Walbart Floral Co.
9727 Clayton Road
St. Louis, MO 63124
314-997-1227

Jon Prell
401 N. Euclid
St. Louis, MO 63108
314-367-4300

Nebraska

Flowers by Simonds
4922 Dodge Street
Omaha, NB 68132
402-558-1155

Ray Gain Florist
4224 Leavenworth
Omaha, NB 68105
405-551-0658

Tyrrell's Flowers of Omaha
107th & Pacific
Shaker Place
Omaha, NB 68114
402-399-9935

New York

The Flower Service
847 Lexington Avenue
New York, NY 10021
212-744-1190

The Green Thumb
    Flowers, Inc.
22 E. 65th Street
New York, NY 10021
212-861-0985

Jennifer A. Ford Associates
146 W. 28th Street
Suite 7E
New York, NY 10001
212-206-7567

Marlo Flowers, Ltd.
421 E. 73rd Street
New York, NY 10021
212-628-2246

Philip Baloun, Design
340 W. 55th Street
New York, NY 10019
212-307-1675

Robert L. Treadway, Design
352 W. 15th Street
New York, NY 10011
212-924-5045

Ronaldo Maia
27 E. 67th Street
New York, NY 10021
212-288-1049

Ohio

Dennis Buttelwerth Florist
2128 Madison Road
Cincinnatti, OH 45208
513-321-3611

Frances Jones Poetker
1037 E. McMillan
Cincinnatti, OH 45206
513-961-6622

Charles M. Phillips, Inc.
13306 Woodland Avenue
Cleveland, OH 44120
216-721-1778

Oregon

Helen's Flowers
5003 N. Lombard Street
Portland, OR 97203
503-285-6908

Tommy Luke
625 SW Morrison Street
Portland, OR 97210
503-228-3131

Pennsylvania

Robinson's Flower Shop
5765 Woodcrest Avenue
Philadelphia, PA 19131
215-879-0566

Rhode Island

The Potted Palm
399 Ives Street
Providence, RI 02906
401-421-8530

South Carolina

Charleston Bouquets
31 E. Battery
Charleston, SC 29401
803-722-2133

Tennessee

The Tulip Tree
6025 Highway 100
Nashville, TN 37205
615-352-1466

Texas

Cowgirls and Flowers
508 Walsh Street
Austin, TX 78703
512-478-4626

Tarry Town Florists
2815 Exposition Boulevard
Austin, TX 78703
512-476-7366

Lee Fritz four Lambert's
7300 Valley View Lane
Dallas, TX 75230
213-239-0121

Bullard's Flowers—David Tiller
4529 McKinney
Dallas, TX 75205
214-528-0383

Zen
2133 Cedar Springs
Dallas, TX 75201
214-871-0383

Flowers on the Square
311 Main
Fort Worth, TX 76102
817-870-2888

Leonard Tharp, Inc.
2705 Bammel
Houston, TX 77098
713-527-9393

The Rose Shop
1903 San Pedro
San Antonio, TX 78212
512-732-1161

Virginia

Ann Wood Carneal
1821 Monument Avenue
Richmond, VA 23220
804-353-5219

Anne Briston
11 Bridgeway Road
Richmond, VA 23226
804-285-2302

Petals
104 N. Wilton Road
Richmond, VA 23226
804-285-8417

Washington

Crissey Flowers & Gifts
2100 5th Avenue
Seattle, WA 98121
206-624-6661

David Adams
89 Virginia
Seattle, WA 98101
206-622-5325

Party Designers

Arizona

Brady's Interior Design &
    Florists
4167 N. Marshall Avenue
Scottsdale, AZ 85019
602-945-8776

California

Parties Plus
3455 S. La Cienega
    Boulevard
Los Angeles, CA 90016
213-838-3800

Dan McCall
300 Donahue Street
Sausalito, CA 94965
415-332-8084

Florida

Harry Bell
460 Worth Avenue
Palm Beach, FL 33480
305-655-6424

Singer & Engelhardt, Inc.
101 Bradley Place
Palm Beach, FL 33480
305-655-6192

Georgia

Dan Carithers, Design
    Consultant
2499 Montview Drive, NW
Atlanta, GA 30305
404-355-8661

Illinois

Marianne Cruikshank
1500 Lake Shore Drive
Chicago, IL 60610
312-951-0777

Jody Elting
810 South Waukegan Road
Lake Forest, IL 60045
312-234-0625

Kentucky

Steve Wilson & Company
1000 Holly Hill Drive
Frankfort, KY 40601
502-875-3224

Missouri

Trapp's
208 Westport Road
Kansas City, MO 64111
816-931-6940

New York

Mark Fahrer Catering
43 W. 13th Street
New York, NY 10011
212-243-6572

Peggy Mulholland
245 E. 37th Street
New York, NY 10016
212-953-9105;
   212-687-3468

Renny Design for
   Entertaining
27 E. 62nd Street
New York, NY 10021
212-371-5354

Rhode Island

Winona Taylor
40 Cranston Avenue
Newport, RI 02840
401-846-7794

Texas

An Affair to Remember, Inc.
4707 Wildwood Road
Dallas, TX 75209
214-357-0013

David Tiller of Bullard's
4529 McKinney
Dallas, TX 75205
214-528-0383

Rosmari Agostini
3201 Drexel Drive
Dallas, TX 75205
214-526-8401

Gourmet Foods by Mail

Florida

Smith Knaupp's Catch of
   the Day
3309 Northeast 33rd Street
Fort Lauderdale, FL 33308
800-327-7723;
   305-565-6619
Fresh stone crab claws

Illinois

Gourmet Fare
4545 S. Racine
Chicago, IL 60609
800-621-0222
*Rainbow trout, lobster tails,
   jumbo shrimp, king crab legs
   and steaks*

Kentucky

Gessemani Farms
Trappist, KY 40051
502-549-3117
Semi-soft chesses

Louisiana

Community Kitchens
P.O. Box 3778
Baton Rouge, LA
   70821-3778
800-535-9901;
   504-381-3900
*Premium coffees and
   gourmet foods*

B. F. Trappey's Sons, Inc.
P.O. Drawer 400
New Iberia, LA 70561-0400
318-365-8281
*Creole and Cajun sauces and
   condiments*

Conrad Rice Mill
307 Ann Street
P.O. Box 296
New Iberia, LA 70560
800-551-3245;
   318-364-7242
*Konriko wild pecan rice,
   artichoke rice mix,
   jambalaya mix, gumbo
   mix, Creole seasoning*

Creole Delicacies Company,
   Inc.
533 St. Ann Street
New Orleans, LA 70116
504-525-9508
*Pecan pralines, praline sauce,
   hot pepper jelly, Creole spices
   and seasonings, New Orleans soups*

Michigan

Fox Hill Farm
444 W. Michigan Avenue
P.O. Box 7
Parma, MI 49269
517-531-3179
Fresh herbs

New York

Flying Foods International
43-44 9th Street
Long Island City, NY 11101
212-706-0820
*Direct source for gourmet deli-
   cacies flown in fresh daily from
   all parts of the world*

Commonwealth Enterprises,
   Ltd.
P.O. Box 49
Mongaup Valley, NY 12762
914-583-6630
Fresh Moulard duck foie gras

Balducci's
424 Sixth Avenue
New York, NY 10011
800-228-2028, extension 72;
   212-673-2600
*Fine foods, including game
   birds, prime meat, fresh produce, cheeses, and caviar*

Pamela Kraussmann's
   Notebooks
496 La Guardia Place
Department 183
New York, NY 10012
212-473-8002
*Sheets of puff pastry; hand-
   made caramels*

Pecos Valley Spice Company
186 Fifth Avenue
New York, NY 10010
212-620-7700
*Ingredients for Mexican
cooking*

Todaro Brothers
557 Second Avenue
New York, NY 10016
212-679-7766
*Fresh Italian cheeses, pastas,
olive oils, mushrooms,
truffles*

Oregon

Harry and David
Bear Creek Orchards
Medford, OR 97501
503-776-2121
*Smoked turkey, salmon, pheasant,
ham, beef brisket, oysters*

Pennsylvania

Walnut Acres, Inc.
Penns Creek, PA 17862
717-837-0601
Home-grown and prepared foods

Vermont

The Cheese House
Route 7A
Arlington, VT 05250
802-375-9033
Cheddar cheeses

Gerard's Haute Cuisine
Main Street
Fairfax, VT 05454
802-849-6141
*Four-star quality gourmet
dinners shipped by air
anywhere in USA*

Washington

Hegg & Hegg
801 Marine Drive
Port Angeles, WA 98362
206-457-3344
*Full sides of boned Puget Sound
salmon smoked over alder
wood*

Further Reading

ANDERSON, JEAN. *Jean Anderson Cooks: Her Kitchen Reference & Recipe Collection.* New York: William Morrow, 1982.

BEARD, JAMES. *Hors d'ouevres and Canapes, Revised Edition.* New York: William Morrow, 1985.

The classic book on food for the cocktail hour. Down-to-earth recipes with sound advice on planning and preparing for cocktail parties of all sorts and sizes.

COLTON, VIRGINIA. *The Joy of Entertaining.* St. Paul: 3M Books, 1983.

Sound advice for the beginner.

COX, BEVERLY. *Cooking Techniques: How to do Anything a Recipe Tells You to Do.* Boston: Little Brown, 1981.

More than 400 techniques explained and illustrated in 2200 clear, close-up photographs.

GINDERS, JAMES. *A Guide to Napkin Folding.* Boston: CBI Publishing, 1980.

HARASZTY, ESZTER. *Living with Flowers: A Comprehensive Guide to Growing and Arranging Flowers.* New York: Liveright (W. W. Norton & Company), 1980.

An informal and relaxed guide to growing and arranging flowers.

KOKKO, MARGO. *The Final Touch: Decorative Garnishes.* Boston: CBI Publishing, 1978.

The Japanese art of carving vegetables, Mukimono. Step-by-step techniques with line art and color photographs show how to create decorative garnishes.

MATTESON, MARILEE. *Simple Feasts: Appetizers, Main Dishes & Desserts.* Boston: Houghton Mifflin, 1983.

MATTESON, MARILEE. *Small Feasts: Soups, Salads & Desserts.* New York: Crown, 1980.

THE MEMPHIS GARDEN CLUB. *The Mid-South Garden Guide.* Jackson: University Press of Mississippi, 1984.

ORTHO BOOKS. *Arranging Cut Flowers.* San Francisco: Chevron Chemical Company, 1985.

OTIS, DENISE, WITH RONALDO MAIA & ERNST BEADLE. *Decorating with Flowers.* New York: Harry N. Abrams Incorporated, 1978.

Standard reference and useful source of ideas from a master flower designer, Ronaldo Maia.

PETERSON, ROGER TORY AND M. MCKENNY. *A Field Guide to Wild Flowers.* Boston: Houghton Mifflin, 1968.

ROHMAN, DALE. *A Time for Flowers.* Gerald, MO: Patrice Press, 1983.

Inspiring photographs of arrangements by flower designer Dale Rohman, pictured in the homes of his St. Louis clients.

STEWART, MARTHA. *Martha Stewart's Hors d'oeuvres: The Creation and Presentation of Fabulous Finger Foods.* New York: Crown, 1984.

TIGERLILY LIMITED. *Flower Arranging*. London: Octopus Books, 1979.

TOZER, ZIBBY. *The Art of Flower Arranging*. New York: Warner Books, 1981.

A charming handbook for the beginner.

WEBB, IRIS, ED. *The Complete Guide to Flower and Foliage Arrangement*. Garden City: Doubleday, 1979.

A comprehensive reference book covering every style of flower arranging from Western traditional to modern, free form and abstract, and the Ikebana school of Japan.

WILLIAMS, SALLIE Y. *American Feasts: The Best of American Regional Cooking*. New York: William Morrow, 1985.

A treasury of over 350 of the best-loved dishes from all points of America's culinary compass.

WILLIAMS, SALLIE Y. *The Art of Presenting Food: A Practical Guide to Food Arrangement and Decoration*. New York: Hearst Books, 1982.

Techniques for decorating and presenting food for the cook who wants to make every dish as appealing to the eye as it is to the palate. Illustrated.

Acknowledgements

Jacket cover photograph: Robert Kirk: catering by Mark Fahrer. **Title page:** Photo by Peter Sanders, Charleston; flowers by Betty Geer of Charleston Bouquets; catering by Cindy Porcher. **Copyright page:** Photo by Peter Sanders, Charleston; flowers by Betty Geer of Charleston Bouquets; catering by Cindy Porcher. **Page 8:** Illustration by Edouardé, from *Chicago History*, published by the Chicago Historical Society. **11:** From *The Gibson Book: A Collection of the Published Works of Charles Dana Gibson*. Vol. I. New York: R. H. Russell and Son, 1906. **13:** Reproduction of painting "Dinner at Haddo House," by A. E. Emslie, courtesy of the National Portrait Gallery, London. **16-17:** Photos by Tony Soluri, Chicago; flowers by Jody Elting of McAdams Florist, Lake Forest. **18-19:** Photos by Carter Smith; flowers by Lulie Cocke; catering by Pat Benton of Blanche's Courtyard, St. Simons Island, Ga., and the Old Edward's Inn, Highlands, N.C. **20-21:** Photos by Bernard Cohen; design by Dan Carithers, with grateful thanks for the advice and cooperation of Lisa B. Newsome, Sally Patterson, Nancy Lynn, Gail Alston, Tootie Benton, and the Piedmont Driving Club of Atlanta, Ga. **22-23:** Photos by Bruce Glassman; flowers by Diana McDermott. We are indebted to Lynden Miller, director of the New York Conservatory Garden, for making the grounds available to us, and for her expert advice on horticultural matters in this book. **24-25:** Photos by Peter Sanders, Charleston; flowers by Betty Geer of Charleston Bouquets; catering by Cindy Porcher. **26-27:** Photo by Dan Barba; mint julep cup photo courtesy of Media Projects Incorporated; flowers by the Green Thumb, New York; bronze sculpture courtesy of the Newmarket Gallery, New York. **28:** Photo courtesy of Media Projects Incorporated. **30:** Photo by Bill Stites, Houston; menu and barn courtesy of San Antonio caterer Don Strange. **32-33:** Photos by Tony Soluri, Chicago; flowers by Jody Elting of McAdams Florist; tea table catered by Patrick Collins, Chicago. **34-35:** Photos by Hank Shull, Darien, Ct. We are indebted to Mrs. Peter Schaaphok for the generous use of her house and treasured family recipes for the annual St. Nicholas' Day Party. **36-37:** Photos courtesy of Media Projects Incorporated. **38:** Photo by Gordon Ingersoll, San Francisco; flowers by Dorothy Deming, Menlowe Park, Cal. **40:** Photo courtesy of Media Projects Incorporated; flowers by Zibby Tozer of the Flower Service, New York. **43:** Photo courtesy of Mark Fahrer, New York. **44-45:** Photo courtesy of Mrs. Leigh Miller, New York. **46:** Photo by Bruce Glassman. **48:** Photo by Peter Sanders, Charleston; Easter rabbit by Betty Geer of Charleston Bouquets; catering by Cindy Porcher. **50:** Photo by Bachrach, courtesy of Kenneth R. Carpenter and Diane De Rosa, New York. **52:** Photo by Dan Barba; flowers by Diana McDermott. **54-55:** Photo by Hickey-Robertson, Houston; flowers by Leonard Tharp, Houston. **56-57:** Photos by Dan Barba; flowers by Diana McDermott. **60:** Photo by Hickey-Robertson, Houston; flowers by Leonard Tharp, Houston. **61:** Photo by Bachrach, courtesy of Kenneth R. Carpenter and Diane De Rosa, New York. **62:** Photo courtesy of David Tiller of Bullard's, Dallas. **63:** Photo by Hickey-Robertson, Houston; flowers by Leonard Tharp, Houston. **64:** Photos by Tony Soluri, Chicago; flowers by Jody Elting of McAdams Florist, Lake Forest. **65:** Lower-left photo by Tony Soluri, Chicago; upper-right photo courtesy of David Tiller of Bullard's, Dallas. **66:** Photos by Allen Mitchell, New Canaan, Ct. **67-68:** Photos by Dan Barba; flowers by Diana McDermott. **69:** Photo by Peter Sanders, Charleston; flowers by Betty Geer, Charleston Bouquets. **70:** Photo by Dan Barba; flowers by Diana McDermott. **72:** Photo by Peter Sanders, Charleston; catering by Cindy Porcher. **75:** Photo courtesy of Media Projects Incorporated. **76:** Photo by Dan Barba; flowers by Diana McDermott. **77:** Photo courtesy of Media Projects Incorporated. **90:** Photo by Tony Soluri, Chicago; flowers by Jody Elting of McAdams Florist, Lake Forest. **92:** Photo by Tony Soluri, Chicago; catering by Patrick Collins, Chicago. **99:** Photo by Jack Wall. **113:** Photos by Peter Sanders, Charleston; catering by Cindy Porcher. **116:** Photo by Dan Barba. Grateful thanks to Angela Weldon and Louise Duncan for their generous assistance and to Charles Patterson, native Kentuckian, for his family recipes. **133:** Photo by Hank Shull, Darien, Ct.; table courtesy of Mrs. Peter Schaaphok. **134:** Photo by Bruce Glassman; table setting courtesy of F. Schumacher & Co. and Gorham; flowers by Diana McDermott. **146:** Photo by Dan Barba; table and menu courtesy of Sallie Y. Williams. **155:** Photo by Carter Smith; catering by Homer McClure, Mobile; flowers by Mary Barney. **157:** Photo by Carter Smith. **158:** Photo courtesy of Media Projects Incorporated. **162:** Photo by Dan Barba; styling by Lloyd Davis; flowers by Diana McDermott. **172:** Photo by Dan Barba; design by Diana McDermott. **183:** Photo by Bruce Glassman; catering by Out of the Woods, New York; flowers by Diana McDermott. **192:** Photo by Hickey-Robertson, Houston; flowers by Leonard Tharp, Houston. **194-195:** Photos by Allan Mitchell, New Canaan, Ct. **201:** Photo by Dan Barba; flowers by Diana McDermott. **203:** Photo by Dan Barba; flowers and line drawings by Diana McDermott. **205:** Photo by Dan Barba; arrangement by Diana McDermott. **206-207:** Photos by Dan Barba; arrangements by Diana McDermott. **208:** Photo by Dan Barba; arrangement by Diana McDermott. **209-210:** Line drawings by Diana McDermott. **212-233:** Line drawings by Diana McDermott.

Index